America's First Ladies

Their Uncommon Wisdom, from Martha Washington to Laura Bush

Edited by
Bill Adler

TAYLOR TRADE PUBLISHING
Lanham • New York • Boulder • Toronto • Oxford

First Taylor Trade Publishing edition 2002

This Taylor Trade Publishing paperback edition of *America's First Ladies* is an original publication. It is published by arrangement with the author.

Designed by David Timmons

Published by Taylor Trade Publishing
An imprint of The Rowman & Littlefield Publishing Group, Inc.
4501 Forbes Boulevard, Suite 200, Lanham, Maryland 20706
Distributed by NATIONAL BOOK NETWORK

The hardback edition of this book was previously cataloged by the Library of Congress.

Library of Congress Cataloging-in-Publication Data

Adler, Bill, 1929–
    America's First Ladies: their uncommon wisdom, from Martha Washington to Laura Bush / Bill Adler.
      p. cm.
    Includes index.
      1. President's spouses—United States—Quotations. 2. Presidents' spouses—United States—Biography. I. Title.

E176.2 .A33 2002
973'.09'9—dc21   2001027502
    ISBN-13: 978-0-87833-273-1 (cloth : alk. paper)
    ISBN-10: 0-87833-273-1 (cloth : alk. paper)
    ISBN-13: 978-1-58979-299-9 (pbk : alk. paper)
    ISBN-10: 1-58979-299-8 (pbk : alk. paper)

Each First Lady is given a magic wand, but
nobody tells her how to use it. Each woman has to
figure that out for herself.

—From Betty Boyd Caroli's
America's First Ladies

CONTENTS

PREFACE

*F*rom the very day we became a nation, Americans have been captivated, enraged, frustrated, and inspired by our First Ladies—long before that title even existed. By 1865 and the end of the Civil War, the wives of U.S. Presidents were highly public figures, in part because of improved magazine distribution across the land. These periodicals carried stories—and sometimes even pictures—of our own "royal" family, and that family's every word, action, and whim was recounted.

It wasn't until the 1880s, however, that the expression "First Lady" came into being. Thus, Lucy Hayes was technically the first First Lady. But even then, the term wasn't part of the national parlance. It took an act of theater to achieve that. A very popular play by Charles Nirdlinger, more or less about Dolley Madison's days as a landlady, bore the title *First Lady*. From then on, so did the Presidents' wives.

Ironically, Jacqueline Kennedy, among the two or three most beloved First Ladies of all time, if not *the most* beloved, never liked the title "First Lady." "It always reminded me of a saddle horse," she said, and she forbade her staff to address her as such. But too many people had used the expression for too long, and Mrs. Kennedy finally had to give in.

Whatever the moniker, the women you are about to meet run quite a remarkable gamut of intelligence, wit, and courage. Both ends of the spectrum are represented, and everything in between as well.

Other writers of books about First Ladies encountered the same problem that we did. In the *Smithsonian Book of the First Ladies: Their Lives, Times, and Issues,* the authors offered the best explanation for this particular problem: "In reading about the first ladies, we discover that very little is known about some of them. It is not unusual for there to be no written records of a woman's life prior to the late nineteenth century. Several factors have made women much less visible than men in our nation's history. For most of this nation's past, 'history' was defined as the lives and deeds of great men whose activities took place in the world of military, economic, or public life. Presidents, politicians, and generals; wars, battles, or major economic changes were what historians (mostly men) wrote about. The details of women's lives—their homes and families, their work in helping their husbands succeed in farming, business, or a career—often were not kept or considered important enough to record."

In fact, some of the First Ladies—especially before women were allowed to vote—were timid and quiet, to say the least. Apparently some of them didn't write letters, or if they did, they were perfunctory. Others, like Bess Truman, destroyed their own and their husbands' letters. Thus, there are some First Ladies for whom only a few good quotes could be found. Indeed, there are several for whom nothing at all of interest has survived. For example, in one case, only a shopping list remains.

A tremendous amount of attention has been lavished on First Ladies Eleanor Roosevelt, Jacqueline Kennedy, and Nancy Reagan. As a result, the trove of their quotations herein is especially rich and meaningful.

Prepare, then, to encounter a seemingly infinite variety of women whose husbands were often, though not always, the most powerful men in the land.

Editor's note: The punctuation, grammar, and spelling have been kept as originally written or spoken. Ellipses are consistent with the source materials.

ACKNOWLEDGMENTS

This book would not have been possible without
the creative assistance of Tom Steele.

MARTHA WASHINGTON

b. 1731   d. 1802

First Lady
APRIL 30, 1789–MARCH 4, 1797

*B*orn June 2, 1731, Martha Dandridge
Custis Washington received very little
formal education, as was the custom in
the eighteenth century. She learned the nuances
of formal entertaining in the upper echelons of
Virginia society as she grew up. Two years after
her first husband died, she married George

Washington. An intensely private person, love of country and love of husband were the only bonds strong enough to pull Mrs. Washington out into the public eye. She summoned all her bravery to support her husband during the Revolutionary War (for instance, she joined him for a time at Valley Forge) and during his term in office as he guided the fledgling nation. Just as General Washington set the standard for future Presidents to follow, Mrs. Washington set a quiet example of the dignity, tact, and hospitality that defines the post of America's First Lady—characteristics that helped her smooth domestic and international diplomatic feathers during the first four years of the new republic.

After stepping out of the glare of the civic spotlight in 1793, Mrs. Washington, always the nurturer, raised two of her grandchildren and one niece at her fabled Mount Vernon home. Mrs. Washington entertained friends, family, and visitors there until her death in 1802. She ensured that her life would remain private by burning her letters before she passed away.

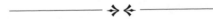

Mrs. Washington left her beloved home and way of life to become First Lady, but she wrote that she had learned from experience that "the greater part of happiness or misery depends on our dispositions and not our circumstances."

She understood her husband's motivations for leading a public life. She wrote, "I cannot blame him for having acted according to his ideas of duty in obeying the voice of his country."

☙

At her husband's insistence, both Mr. and Mrs. Washington led daily lives filled with restrictions. "I lead a very dull life [as First Lady]," she wrote her sister, "and know nothing of what passes in the town. I never go to any public place, indeed I think I am more like a state prisoner than anything else. There [are] certain bounds set for me which I must not depart from and as I cannot do as I like I am obstinate [and] stay at home a great deal."

☙

From the temporary capital, New York, she wrote to her niece, "I have not had one half hour to myself. . . . My hair is set and dressed every day and I have put on white muslin habits for the summer."

☙

She never canceled an engagement: "I have been so long accustomed to conform to events which are governed by public voice that I hardly dare indulge any personal wishes which cannot yield to that."

☙

Mrs. Washington stated that her husband had

"impressed her with his views so thoroughly that she could not distinguish her own."

❧

When asked about British-American relations after the Revolutionary War, she commented, "The difficulties and distresses to which we have been exposed during the war must now be forgotten. We must endeavor to let our ways be the way of pleasantness and all our paths Peace."

❧

Mrs. Washington thanked a friend for a sincere letter that gave her "more satisfaction than all the formal compliments and empty ceremonies of mere etiquette. I am only fond of what comes from the heart. . . . The difficulties which presented themselves . . . entering upon the Presidency seem thus to be in some measure surmounted . . . my new and unwished-for situation is not indeed a burden to me. . . . I sometimes think the arrangement is not quite as it ought to have been; that I, who had much rather be at home, should occupy a place which a great many younger and gayer women would be prodigiously pleased."

She put forth a rather passive philosophy on the role. "I do not . . . feel dissatisfied with my present situation. No. God forbid! For everybody and everything conspire to make me as contented as possible in it. Yet I know too much of the vanity of human affairs to expect felicity from the splendid scenes of public life. I am still determined to be cheerful and to be happy, in whatever situation I may be; for I have also learned from experience that the greater part of our happiness or misery depends upon our dispositions, and not upon our circumstances."

❧

Martha Washington was an adamantly proud American. As she told a friend returning from Europe, "That you arrived from Europe with all your prejudices in favor of America I have no doubt, for I think our country affords everything that can give pleasure or satisfaction to a rational mind."

❧

Something of a feminist, she believed strongly that women needed to exercise independence. She wrote a young niece: "There are few people that can manage more than their own business. I very sincearly wish you would exert yourself so as to keep all your matters in order yourself without depending on others as that is the only way to be happy—to have all your business in your own hands without trusting to others. . . . Look upon this advice in the friendly way it is meant, as I wish you to be as independent as your circumstances will admit and to be so, is to exert yourself in the management of your estate. If you do not no one else will. A dependence is, I think, a wretched state and you have enough if you will manage it right."

❧

Unfortunately, she was also a racist, as were most Americans of any station at the time. "Black children are liable to so many accidents and complaints that one is heartily sore of keeping them. I hope you will not find in him much sass. The Blacks are so bad in their nature that they have not the least gratitude for the kindness that may be shown them. . . . The women that wash, they always idle half their time away about their own business and wash so bad that the clothes are not fit to use."

჻

"Though I may not have a great deal of business of consequence, I have a great many avocations of one kind or another which imperceptibly consume my time."

჻

The day before Mrs. Washington left First Ladyship, she wrote to a friend that the "winter had been very severe here, and upon the whole dull; but it is now moderating and drawing to a close, with which the curtain will fall on our public life, and place us on a more tranquil theater."

჻

She enjoyed her retirement from public life: "New York and Philadelphia was not home, only a sojourning," she told a friend, adding that she felt like a child "just released from a taskmaster." She felt "steady as a clock, busy as a bee, and cheerful as a cricket."

ABIGAIL ADAMS

b. 1744   d. 1818

First Lady

MARCH 4, 1797–MARCH 4, 1801

Abigail Smith Adams brought natural charm, a sharp intellect, a prestigious pedigree, polished rules of decorum, and experience to her role as First Lady. Born in 1744 into one of the oldest families in America, Mrs. Adams learned the art of entertaining at a young age. However, after marrying John Adams, she had to run the family farm, educate her children, and contend with food and supply shortages while he was away during the Revolutionary War and while he was assigned to other positions throughout the years. Her letters describe her loneliness during this time. "Alas!" she wrote in the winter of 1773. "How many snow banks divide thee and me."

Mrs. Adams perfected her social skills in 1784 while her husband served briefly at a diplomatic post in Paris and later as the first United States Minister to Great Britain. To the formal court entertaining that she learned abroad, she added her experience as Martha Washington's right-hand woman when Mrs. Adams was the Vice President's wife. She was able to prevail over the primitive conditions at the new capitol and thus maintained the country's dignity as it sought to enter the ranks of international ruling powers.

Mrs. Adams read avidly despite her lack of formal education. Her passion for learning equaled her husband John's, and they built their fifty-two-year marriage on a foundation of love and respect for knowledge. Though she spent more than half of her married life separated from her husband, her prolific letters—sometimes satirical, sometimes forceful—kept them connected and infused their intellectual discourse with intensity. Mrs. Adams held strong political views of her own, and her insightful opinion often influenced her husband's decisions and guided his career. The couple enjoyed seventeen years of life together after retiring from civic duties until her death in 1818.

Mrs. Adams was every inch as dedicated to the cause of this nation's independence as her husband was, and she had quite a vivid and eloquent vision of what that independent nation should look like. In 1776, when Mr. Adams joined the Founding Fathers in Philadelphia to charter the future of the new democracy by writing the Constitution, Mrs. Adams wrote from their home in Braintree, Massachusetts, to describe the condition of wartime Boston, as well as to proffer advice to the Continental Congress. In her letter, she rebuked the Earl of Dunmore (the Governor of Virginia, who actually ended up taking Britain's side in the war). She also asked that her husband and his colleagues "remember the ladies" as they began to formulate the Declaration of Independence. It is for this plea that Mrs. Adams is perhaps best remembered. Here is the full text of her famous letter, with contemporaneous spelling and grammar left as written:

BRAINTREE, MARCH 31, 1776

I wish you would ever write me a Letter half as long as I write you; and tell me if you may where your Fleet are gone? What sort of Defence Virginia can make against our common Enemy? Whether it is so situated as to make an able Defence? Are not the Gentery Lords and the common people vassals? Are they not like the uncivilized Natives Brittain represents us to be? I hope their Riffel Men, who have shewn themselves very savage and even Blood thirsty, are not a specimen of the Generality of the people.

I am willing to allow the Colony great merrit for having produced a Washington, but they have been shamefully duped by a Dunmore.

I have sometimes been ready to think that the passion for Liberty cannot be Equally Strong in the Breasts of those who have been accustomed to deprive their fellow Creatures of theirs. Of this I am certain: that it is not founded upon the generous and christian principal of doing to others as we would that others should do unto us.

Do not you want to see Boston; I am fearful of the small pox, or I should have been in before this time. I got Mr. Crane to go to our House and see what state it was in. I find it has been occupied by one of the Doctors of a Regiment, very dirty, but no other damage has been done to it. The few things which were left in it are all gone. Crane has the key, which he never delivered up. I have wrote to him for it and am deter-mined to get it cleaned as soon as possible and shut it up. I look upon it a new acquisition of property, a property which one month ago I did not value at a single Shilling, and could with pleasure have seen it in flames.

The Town in General is left in a better state than we expected, more oweing to a percipitate flight than any Regard to the inhabitants, tho some individuals discovered a sense of honour and justice and have left the rent of the Houses in which they were for the owners and the furniture unhurt, or if damaged sufficient to make good.

Others have committed abominable Ravages. The Mansion House of your President is safe and the furniture unhurt, whilst both the House and the Furniture of the Solisiter General have fallen a prey to their own merciless party. Surely the very Fiends feel a Reverential awe for Virtue and patriotism, whilst they Detest the paricide and traitor.

I feel very differently at the approach of spring to which I did a month ago. We knew not then whether we could plant or sow with safety, whether when we had toiled we could reap the fruits of our own industry, whether we could rest in our own Cottages, or whether we should not be driven from the sea coasts to seek shelter in the wilderness, but now we feel as if we might sit under our own vine and eat the good of the land.

I feel a *gaieti de Coar* [gladness of the

heart] to which before I was a stranger. I
think the Sun looks brighter, the Birds sing
more melodiously, and Nature puts on a
more chearfull countanance. We feel a temporary peace, and the poor fugitives are
returning to their deserted habitations.

Tho we felicitate ourselves, we sympa-
thize with those who are trembling least the
Lot of Boston should be theirs. But they cannot be in similar circumstances unless pusi-
lanimity and cowardise should take possession of them. They have time and warning
given to them to see the Evil and shun it.—I
long to hear that you have declared an inde-
pendency—and by the way, in the new Code
of Laws which I suppose it will be necessary
for you to make, I desire you would Remember the Ladies, and be more generous and
favourable to them than your ancestors. Do
not put such unlimited power into the hands
of the Husbands. Remember, all Men would
be tyrants if they could. If perticular care and
attention is not paid to the Ladies, we are
determined to foment a Rebelion, and will
not hold ourselves bound by any Laws in
which we have no voice, or Representation.

That your Sex are Naturally Tyrannical
is Truth so thoroughly established as to admit
no dispute, but such of you as wish to be
happy willingly give up the harsh title of
Master for the more tender and endearing
one of Friend. Why, then, not put it out of the

power of the vicious and the Lawless to use
us with cruelty and indignity with impunity.
Men of Sense in all Ages abhor those customs
which treat us only as the vassals of your Sex.
Regard us then as Beings placed by providence under your protection, and in immita-
tion of the Supreem Being, make use of that
power only for our happiness.

ABIGAIL

❧

Clearly a feminist, Mrs. Adams insisted, "I will
never consent to have our Sex considered in an
inferior point of light."

❧

"No man ever prospered in the world without
the consent and cooperation of his wife."

❧

During a particularly hot August, Mrs. Adams
wrote from Philadelphia to her sister in London of
the tribulations of social obligations: "I have been
fully employed in entertaining company, in the
first place all the Senators who had ladies and
families, then the remaining senators and this
week we have begun with the House, and tho we
have a room in which we dine 24 persons at a
time, I shall not get through them all with the
public Ministers for a month to come. . . . The
weather is so warm that we can give only one dinner a week. I cannot find a cook in the whole city
but what will get drunk."

❧

On her husband's inauguration day, Mrs.
Adams was still up in Quincy. She wrote to him:
"My feelings are not those of pride or ostentation,
upon the occasion. They are . . . a sense of the
obligation, the important trusts, and numerous
duties connected with it." As for herself, she felt
she should probably emulate her predecessor,
though she said she'd rather be bound and gagged
and shot like a turkey. "As to a crown . . . I shall
esteem myself peculiarly fortunate, if, at the close
of my public life, I can retire esteemed, beloved,
and equally respected with my predecessor."

❧

By 1800, the White House, although basically
livable, was still under construction and located in
what amounted to a frontier. Mrs. Adams wrote to
her daughter Abigail: "To assist us in this great
castle and render less attendance necessary, bells
are wholly wanting . . . and promises are all you
can obtain. This is so great an inconvenience that
I know not what to do or how to do . . . if they will
put me up some bells and let me have wood
enough to keep fires, I design to be pleased. I
could content myself almost anywhere three
months, but surrounded with forests, can you
believe that wood is not to be had, because people
cannot be found to cut and cart it! . . . We have
indeed, come into a new country. . . . You must

keep all this to yourself and when asked how I like it, say that I write you the situation is beautiful which is true. The house is made habitable but there is not a single apartment finished. . . . If the twelve years in which this place has been considered as the future seat of government had been improved as they would have been in New England, very many of the present inconveniences would have been removed."

⤳

Speaking her mind in public was Mrs. Adams's primary fear: "I have been so used to freedom of sentiment that I know not how to place so many guards about me, as will be indispensable, to look at every word before I utter it, and to impose a silence upon myself, when I long to talk."

⤳

Although she blamed Thomas Jefferson for leading the opposition that criticized her husband's leadership and ousted him from office after only one term, Mrs. Adams couldn't bring herself to renounce their former friendship. To her son, she said, "There is a little corner of my heart where he once sat as a friend."

⤳

Toward the end of her life, Mrs. Adams wrote, "I am determined to be very well pleased with the world, and wish well to all its inhabitants. Altho in my journey through it, I meet with some who are

too selfish, others too ambitious, some uncharita-
ble, others malicious and envious, yet these vices
are counterbalanced. . . . I always thought the
laughing phylosopher a much wiser man, than the
sniveling one."

DOLLEY MADISON

b. 1768   d. 1849

First Lady
MARCH 4, 1801–MARCH 4, 1809;
MARCH 4, 1809–MARCH 4, 1817

Dorothea "Dolley" Payne Todd Madison's world-famous hospitality made her one of the best-loved social figures of her time. She acted as Thomas Jefferson's First Lady for eight years. Then, beginning with her official instatement as First Lady at the first-ever inaugural ball, which was held for her husband James, she continued as the social leader of the country. Mrs. Madison elevated the post of First Lady to new heights with her queenly fashions and lavish Southern style of entertainment.

During the War of 1812, Mrs. Madison was forced to draw on the inner strength provided by her Quaker background. She proved herself level-headed in adverse conditions when she saved Gilbert Stuart's famous portrait of George Washington from destruction as she fled the British advance on the White House. The war left the White House in ruins, but Mrs. Madison perse-vered and continued entertaining her guests at temporary locations. After her term as First Lady, the beloved Mrs. Madison continued to be the hub of society until her death in 1849.

Mrs. Madison's largesse as a hostess was immor-talized by the aggrieved wife of the British Minister, who said that a meal at the Madisons' was "more like a harvest home supper than the entertainment of a Secretary of State." Mrs. Madison replied as pleasantly as possible, "The profusion of my table so repugnant to foreign cus-toms arises from the happy circumstance of abun-dance and prosperity in our country, and I shall continue to prefer Virginia liberality to European elegance."

"There is one secret, and that is the power we all have in forming our own destinies."

꩜

A seamstress told a White House decorator that Mrs. Madison disliked his work for her. Made aware that her comments had been disclosed, but not knowing who had told the decorator, Mrs. Madison wrote him quite an icy note: "The varnished tale . . . of . . . my conduct . . . has been insufficient to assure your judgment . . . and as it is one of my sources of happiness never to desire a knowledge of other people's business . . . I shall be strict in my examination of the servants. . . . I wish to know those who have taken the liberty to misrepresent me."

꩜

During the War of 1812, when the British invaded Washington, Mrs. Madison refused to join the panicking, fleeing throngs, despite the fact that both the President and the Mayor of Washington commanded her to do so. "I was so unfeminine as to be free from fear," she later recalled. She refused to budge until the sound of nearby cannon fire got too close for comfort.

ELIZABETH MONROE

b. 1768   d. 1830

First Lady
MARCH 4, 1817–MARCH 4, 1825

Though Elizabeth Kortright Monroe's entertaining style was much more formal and reserved than her predecessor Dolley Madison's, Mrs. Monroe's life was filled with romance and adventure. Her father assisted the British during the French and Indian Wars and did not participate in the Revolutionary

War, so young Elizabeth must have been madly in love indeed to have married the patriot James Monroe in 1786 when she was seventeen. She accompanied her husband while he served in various political capacities abroad, including time in Paris during the French Revolution when he was the United States Minister. Mrs. Monroe went to the Parisian prison where the Marquis de Lafayette's wife was awaiting the guillotine to see the alleged criminal. Such expressed American interest in Madame Lafayette brought about the prisoner's release, and thus Mrs. Monroe single-handedly saved the Frenchwoman's life. Thereafter, Mrs. Monroe was a favorite among the grateful French, who called her *la belle Américaine.*

During Mrs. Monroe's eight-year term as First Lady, failing health did not permit her to reciprocate social calls, which was sometimes thought an offense within the intricate rules of etiquette among visiting diplomats' wives. However, Mrs. Monroe emulated the elaborate manner of hostessing popular in Europe and in New York for White House social functions. Her daughter Maria was the first daughter of a President to be married in the White House, but the "New York" style ceremony was private and exclusive. After retiring, the former First Lady lived a quiet life with her family at the Virginia mansion until her death in 1830.

Louisa Adams

b. 1775   d. 1852

First Lady
MARCH 4, 1825–MARCH 4, 1829

ondon-born Louisa Catherine Johnson Adams was the only First Lady to have been born outside of America, but because her father was American, she was a United States citizen. She was raised abroad and did not come to the United States until 1801, four years after she married the quick-tempered diplomat John Quincy Adams. After years among courtly elegance, the rough-and-ready ways of her "home" country that she found in New England shocked her sensibilities. Mrs. Adams adjusted much more readily to her Washington residence.

In 1809 she followed Mr. Adams to Russia with their two-year-old son and was again immersed in the grandeur of noble living. However, her husband's small salary as Minister did not sufficiently support the requirements of such high living, and that, along with the extreme cold, culture shock, and Mrs. Adams's failing health, made the time in Russia a trial. Mr. Adams was transferred to London, but in order to join him Mrs. Adams had to travel across war-torn countries by coach for forty days. Two years later, they moved back to Washington, where the couple's drawing-room parties were a center of arts and entertainment.

After becoming First Lady in 1825, however, Mrs. Adams became depressed by the strain of the election and her failing health. She continued entertaining despite her difficulties, and she even managed to devote time and effort to furnish some of the White House rooms that her mother-in-law Abigail had found so barren years before. After her four years in the White House, Mrs. Adams continued to live the life of a politician's wife while Mr. Adams served seventeen years in Congress. The couple lived to celebrate their fiftieth wedding anniversary before John died in 1848. Mrs. Adams survived her husband by four years and was then buried next to him at his family home in Quincy, Massachusetts.

Mrs. Adams wrote to her father-in-law, former President John Adams, in 1819: "The woman selected for your wife [Abigail Adams] was so highly gifted in mind, with powers so vast, and such quick and clear perception, altogether so superior to the general run of females, you have perhaps formed a too-enlarged opinion of the capacities of our sex, and having never witnessed their frailties, are not aware of the dangers to which they are exposed, by acquirements above their strength."

"Hanging and marriage were strongly assimilated."

"I have nothing to do with the disposal of affairs and have never but once been consulted."

"The more I bear, the more is expected to me, and I sink in the efforts I make to answer such expectations."

"I was carried through my journey and trials by the mercy of a kind Providence, and by the conviction that weakness, either of body or mind, would only render my difficulties greater and make matters worse."

～✦～

Mrs. Adams joined what would become a succession of First Ladies who loathed the White House. "There is something in this great unsocial house which depresses my spirits beyond expression and makes it impossible for me to feel at home or to fancy that I have a home any where."

～✦～

Elsewhere, she referred to the White House as "that dull and stately prison in which the sounds of mirth are seldom heard."

～✦～

Dolley Madison had initiated the custom of calling on the wives of all the legislators who lived in Washington—a custom her successors despised. Mrs. Madison's successor, Elizabeth Monroe, could legitimately plead poor health and avoid these visits, but Mrs. Adams had no such luck. While John Quincy Adams served as Secretary of State, he enlisted Mrs. Adams's help in getting him into the White House by preparing, each morning, a list of homes for her to visit. She wrote that he fashioned those lists "as carefully as a commercial treaty." In her diary, she wrote with acerbity, "It is understood that a man who is ambitious to become President of the United States must make his wife visit the Ladies of the members of

Congress first. Otherwise he is totally inefficient to fill so high an office. . . . These visits have made me sick many times, and I really sometimes think they will make me crazy."

⌇

A passive, forlorn sort of feminist, Louisa Adams once wrote in an angry letter to her husband, "That sense of inferiority which by nature and by law we are compelled to feel and to which we must submit is worn by us with as much satisfaction as the badge of slavery generally, and we love to be flattered out of our sense of degradation."

⌇

When she wrote her life story for her children, she self-deprecatingly called it "Adventures of a Nobody."

Rachel Jackson

b. 1767   d. 1828

First Lady
DIED BEFORE INAUGURATION, SEVEN WEEKS
AFTER ELECTION

Rachel Donelson Robards Jackson's first husband was unbearably jealous, so they separated after six years when she was twenty-three. She was under the impression that he was filing for divorce. She married Andrew Jackson in 1791, but two years into their happy marriage, they discovered that Mrs. Jackson was still Mrs. Robards; her first husband had not ever really divorced her. Mr. Robards vengefully charged his wife and Mr. Jackson with adultery and finally obtained a divorce. Although Mr. Jackson's was an honest mistake, the press and his political opponents attacked him and his wife mercilessly. The rumors hurt her dreadfully, and Mr. Jackson blamed himself for not checking the records more carefully. After he was elected President, Mrs. Jackson said that she didn't want to live in the White House. She died of a heart attack in 1828 between the election and the inauguration and was buried in her inaugural gown.

Twenty-one-year-old Emily Donelson, one of Mrs. Jackson's favorite nieces, served as First Lady for a portion of Mr. Jackson's presidency. Though in fragile health, Mrs. Donelson had the courage to argue points of principle with the President and the strength to bear three children before her death from tuberculosis in 1836. Sarah Yorke Jackson, Mr. Jackson's daughter-in-law, served as the White House hostess until the end of President Jackson's second term.

Mrs. Jackson was among the most devoutly religious women ever to serve as First Lady. She wrote to a friend:

To tell you of this city [Washington], I would not do justice to the subject. The extravagance is in dressing and running to parties; but I must say they regard the Sabbath, and attend preaching, for there are churches of every denomination and able ministers of the gospel. . . .

Oh, my dear friend, how shall I get through this bustle? There are not less than from fifty to one hundred persons calling in a day. My dear husband was unwell nearly the whole of our journey, but, thanks to our Heavenly Father, his health is improving. . . .

Don't be afraid of my giving way to . . . vain things. The apostle says, I can do all things in Christ, who strengtheneth me. The play-actors sent me a letter, requesting my countenance to them. No. A ticket to balls and parties. No. Not one. Two dinings; several times to drink tea. Indeed, Mr. Jackson encourages me in my course. He recommends it to me to be steadfast. I am going to-day to hear Mr. Summerfield. He preaches in the Methodist church; a very highly spoken of minister. Glory to God for the privilege. Not a day or not but there is the church opened for prayer.

ᘐ

Another obvious fan of the White House, Mrs. Jackson once declared: "I had rather be a doorkeeper in the house of God than live in that palace at Washington."

చ్య

Rachel Jackson's epitaph read, "A being so gentle and so virtuous slander might wound, but could not dishonor."

Anna Harrison

b. 1775   d. 1864

First Lady
MARCH 4, 1841–APRIL 14, 1841

After growing up in refined East Coast society, Anna Tuthill Symmes Harrison moved to Ohio with her father. Soon thereafter, in 1795, she married Lieutenant William Henry Harrison without her father's permission. Though her father did not want her to lead the life of a soldier's wife, he eventually approved because she was so happy. Mr.

Harrison's performances in the War of 1812 were legendary. Mrs. Harrison wanted him to retire after years of risking his life on the frontier; she accepted his move into the political arena only because she understood how strong his ambition was to become President.

After the inauguration, President Harrison's daughter-in-law served as White House hostess while Anna Harrison made arrangements for the move to Washington. She was packing for the trip to join her husband when she heard the news of his death from pneumonia, only one month into his term. Mrs. Harrison died in 1864 at the age of eighty-eight.

Mrs. Harrison opposed her husband's candidacy. "I wish that my husband's friends had left him where he is, happy and contented in retirement."

Mrs. Harrison was distinctly displeased the first time she saw the White House. "We are here for four years," she said. "I do not look beyond that, as many things may occur in that time, but I am very anxious to see the family of the President provided for properly, and while I am here I hope to be able to get the present building put into good condition. Very few people understand to what straits the President's family has been put at times for lack of accommodations. Really there are only five sleep-ing apartments and there is no feeling of privacy."

JULIA TYLER

b. 1820   d. 1889

First Lady
JUNE 26, 1844–MARCH 4, 1845

*J*ulia *Gardiner Tyler* was a beautiful, genteel young woman who enchanted society after her debut in 1835 at the age of fifteen. Five years later she was known as the "Rose of Long Island." President John Tyler, a widower thirty years her senior, was among her admirers. He won her hand after she accompanied him on a trip on a new steam frigate; her father died during the trip and the President comforted her so successfully that he won her over and she consented to marry him. The first President to marry in office generated a great deal of publicity, and his second wife's young age, twenty-four, raised some eyebrows. However, the 1844 marriage proved a success. The training she received as a wealthy debutante helped the new First Lady earn respect as a capable and charming hostess during her eight-month reign at the helm of Washington society.

After Mr. Tyler's term ended, the couple retired to their Virginia plantation until the Civil War broke out. Mrs. Tyler remained devoted to her husband even after his death in 1862. She agreed with his political views—supporting slavery and states' rights—and did volunteer work for the Confederacy during the war while she was a refugee in New York. After the war, she lobbied Congress to create a law to allow a pension for the widows of Presidents. Congress eventually did pass such a law, which greatly alleviated Mrs. Tyler's financial problems. She died in Richmond, Virginia, in 1889.

———————— ✦✦ ————————

President Tyler was thirty years older than his wife, but she did not see this as a problem. Mrs. Tyler noted that John Tyler seemed "more agreeable in every way than any young man ever was or ever could be."

༄

"I have commenced my auspicious reign,"
Mrs. Tyler wrote sarcastically, "and am in quiet
possession of the Presidential Mansion. . . . This
winter I intend to do something in the way of
entertaining that shall be the admiration and talk
of all the Washington world."

༄

According to Mrs. Tyler, "Nothing appears to
delight the President more than . . . to hear people
sing my praises."

༄

Mrs. Tyler wrote a poem to her husband on his
sixtieth birthday, saying, "what e'er changes time
may bring, I'll love thee as thou art!"

Sarah Polk

b. 1803   d. 1891

First Lady
MARCH 4, 1845–MARCH 4, 1849

The privileged child of a wealthy family, Sarah Childress Polk was formally educated in Nashville, Tennessee, and in Salem, North Carolina, at the Moravian Institute's female academy, which provided one of the few opportunities for higher education for nineteenth-century women. During her marriage to James K. Polk,

Mrs. Polk combined her intellectual abilities with her social skills to assist the President's career. Mrs. Polk privately advised her husband and helped him write speeches and political correspondence. Sometimes when she would remind him not to work too hard, he would change the subject by handing her a newspaper and saying, "Sarah, here is something I wish you to read."

A devout Presbyterian, Mrs. Polk did not attend the theater or horse racing and did not allow dancing or drinking in the White House. However, her insightful and engaging conversation delighted guests and solidified her reputation as an enchanting hostess. Mr. Polk died at the couple's Nashville home only three months after leaving office. Mrs. Polk, always dressed in black, kept the house as a memorial to her husband for forty-two years. It was accepted as neutral ground during the Civil War, and leaders from both the gray and the blue visited "Polk Place" to honor the former President. Mrs. Polk died in 1891 at the age of eighty-eight.

Although famous for her personal and social austerity—she banished alcohol and fancy dinners from the White House, rigidly observed the Sabbath, and did not dance—Mrs. Polk was well liked. Tolerant of those who did not share her rigid notions, she was prone to pardon them with the observation, "You were not brought up in so strict a school as I was."

✧

"If I get to the White House, I will neither keep house nor make butter."

✧

"To dance in these [White House] rooms would be undignified," Mrs. Polk once explained as gently as possible. "How indecorous it would seem for dancing to be going on in one apartment, while in another we were conversing with dignitaries of the republic or ministers of the gospel."

✧

The man her husband had defeated in the presidential election, Henry Clay, once gallantly told Mrs. Polk that he could not help approving of *her* administration as First Lady. He added, however, that there was some difference of opinion about her husband's administration. She thanked him for his double-edged compliment and said, "If a political opponent of my husband is to succeed him I have always said I prefer you, Mr. Clay, and in that event I shall be most happy to surrender the White House to you."

✧

"I always take a deep interest in State and national affairs."

✧

Sarah Polk believed that God had preordained her life (and everyone else's): "The greater the prosperity the deeper the sense of gratitude to the Almighty. . . . My heart never yielded to worldly honors or self-vanity. . . . I recognize nothing in myself; I am only an atom in the hands of God."

MARGARET TAYLOR

b. 1788   d. 1852

First Lady
MARCH 4, 1849–JULY 9, 1850

$\mathfrak{M}$argaret "Peggy" Mackall Smith Taylor followed her husband, General Zachary Taylor, as he moved around to many different outposts and forts on the Western frontier. Despite her genteel upbringing, she bore the hardships of rough outdoor life valiantly. However, she violently opposed the idea of her husband taking the nomination for President. Mrs. Taylor did not participate in any formal social functions after his election. She lived a quiet, private life in the White House, entertaining only close friends and family and attending church regularly.

Mrs. Taylor's youngest daughter, Mary Elizabeth Taylor Bliss, who was called "Betty," served as her father's official hostess at White House functions in place of her mother. After only fifteen months in office, President Taylor died, fulfilling his wife's prediction that the hard work of his job would shorten his life. Mrs. Taylor then retired to Kentucky, where she died in 1852.

By the time Zachary Taylor was President, Mrs. Taylor's health was poor. She died a very bitter woman indeed. Her last words were to reassure a worried niece: "My dear, do not trouble yourself about it; there is nothing in *this* world worth caring for."

ABIGAIL FILLMORE

b. 1798   d. 1853

First Lady

JULY 9, 1850–MARCH 4, 1853

Abigail Powers Fillmore worked as a
schoolteacher while her prospective husband, Millard Fillmore, worked to
become a lawyer. She continued working after the
marriage, and thus became the first First Lady to
claim such a distinction. Even after she quit working, after her husband became a successful lawyer
and entered the political arena, frontier-raised

Mrs. Fillmore continued to read avidly. When Vice President Fillmore became President after Zachary Taylor died unexpectedly in 1850, Abigail Fillmore was elevated to the post of First Lady. Mrs. Fillmore's love of reading served her well when she took it upon herself to select books to fill the shelves of the White House library.

Unfortunately, a debilitating permanent ankle injury and overall poor health kept Mrs. Fillmore from participating fully in Washington's lively social scene. Preferring the solace of her books and music to the more harrowing tasks of a First Lady, Mrs. Fillmore let her daughter Abby preside over routine social duties in her stead. But despite her pain, she attended all official dinners and events. Her sense of duty led Mrs. Fillmore to insist on standing at her place by her husband's side at Franklin Pierce's inaugural ceremony in inclement weather. As a result, she caught pneumonia and died a few weeks later in 1853.

An early letter reveals a certain intensity in her relationship with Mr. Fillmore: "I have spent the day at home," she wrote to him. "Have felt more than usual lonely tho' not unhappy or discontented. Your society is all I have thought of."

In another letter, she told him she was "happy and proud in the thought that your heart is firm, and that no fascinating female can induce you to forget whose whole heart is devoted."

JANE PIERCE

b. 1806   d. 1863

First Lady
MARCH 4, 1853–MARCH 4, 1857

*J*ane Means Appleton Pierce endured personal tragedies, persevered despite ill health, and suffered through her husband's political career, which she did not approve of. Mrs. Pierce tried to discourage Franklin Pierce's ambitions to enter into civic life. During his time as a U.S. Senator, the couple had two sons, both of whom died in infancy. After Mr. Pierce returned from the Mexican War, Mrs. Pierce enjoyed four happy years with her husband and their third son Benjamin, called "Benny." When Pierce received the nomination for President in 1852, his wife immediately fainted. The news shattered Mrs. Pierce's peaceful life in New Hampshire, and it seemed that every event from that point forward only added to her unhappiness.

Mrs. Pierce was completely opposed to her husband's bid for the presidency, but he convinced her that it was best for their son's future. While traveling by train, however, the family's car derailed and both parents saw their son Benny die. The inauguration took place two months later under a cloud of mourning without the presence of Mrs. Pierce. That month, former First Lady Fillmore died, and Vice President Rufus King passed away one month later. Mrs. Pierce did not have the strength to attend very many social functions and was assisted as much as possible by friends. After retirement, the Pierces traveled abroad, looking for a health-inspiring climate for the former First Lady, but nothing helped. They returned to New Hampshire, where Mrs. Pierce died in 1863.

Mrs. Pierce once wrote home to New Hampshire: "Oh, how I wish [Franklin Pierce] was out of political life! How much better it would be for him on every count!"

ॐ

On her impending role as First Lady: "If what seems so probably is to come I pray that grace may be given where it is and will be much so needed."

ॐ

Mrs. Pierce never really recovered from her son's tragic death. In her darkened room, she wrote letters to her dead son, asking his forgiveness. She wrote her sister, "The last two nights my dear boy has been in my dreams with peculiar vividness. May God forgive this aching yearning I feel so much. . . . Mr. Pierce is burdened with cares and perplexities. . . . He has but three large dinners yet, at all of which I have appeared, but not at the evening [public] receptions. . . . Little interruptions are very abundant here, and I do not accomplish half I wish to, either in reading or writing. . . . I came accidentally upon some of my precious child's things . . . but I was obliged to turn and seem interested in *other things*."

MARY TODD LINCOLN

b. 1818   d. 1882

First Lady
MARCH 4, 1861–APRIL 15, 1865

a diminutive fireball, Mary Ann Todd
Lincoln could not have been more different from her tall (fourteen inches taller!),
deliberate husband, Abraham. Yet their boundless
love softened the edges of these differences so
much that the President was once heard to say,
"My wife is as handsome as when she was a girl,

and I . . . fell in love with her; and what is more, I have never fallen out." Mrs. Lincoln was raised to charm the elite circles of society in Lexington, Kentucky, but after she moved to Springfield, Illinois, at the age of twenty-one, she began a tempestuous courtship (that included a broken engagement) with her future husband, who was not well-off at the time. Her faith in her husband's ability to be something great gave her the strength to endure years without the finery and society that she was accustomed to.

Mrs. Lincoln's confidence was justified in 1860 when Lincoln was elected President. However, the elevated social position of First Lady brought criticism and sadness to Mrs. Lincoln. Southerners called her a traitor during the Civil War, and Northerners resented her excessive spending during impulsive shopping sprees. In entertaining guests, she was accused of wastefulness, and after she stopped entertaining to mourn her son Willie's death, she was rebuked for neglecting her duties as First Lady.

Mrs. Lincoln spent a great deal of time comforting and raising money for injured soldiers. But after the end of the war and her husband's assassination in 1865, she was overwhelmed by unhappiness and wandered Europe aimlessly as she became more and more destitute. Her beloved son Tad died in 1871, sending her in a tailspin to an even deeper depression. Her oldest son Robert arranged for an insanity trial, where she was convicted. After a few months in Bellevue, a sanitarium, she was found sane in another trial. Thereafter she again traveled Europe, seeking cures for her undiagnosed diabetes, spinal arthritis, and migraines. Mrs. Lincoln died at the age of sixty-three, possibly from a stroke. The wedding ring that she was buried with, although worn and thin, still read "Love is Eternal."

Mrs. Lincoln often told of the first time she met her husband, at a social event. Mr. Lincoln approached, introduced himself, and said, "I want to dance with you in the worst way." After a stultifying turn around the floor, she remarked that he must have meant "in the *very* worst way."

Initially, Mrs. Lincoln enjoyed her role as First Lady: "how every moment is occupied. . . . This certainly is a charming spot . . . every evening our blue room is filled with the elite of the land. . . . I am beginning to feel so perfectly at home, and enjoy every thing so much."

Mrs. Lincoln lived in perpetual terror of her husband discovering that she was, in fact, among the most extravagant of all First Ladies when it came to her wardrobe. During Mr. Lincoln's reelection campaign, she told a friend, "I do not know what would become of us all. If he is reelected I can keep him in ignorance of my

affairs; but if he is defeated, then the bills will be
sent in and he will know all."

⌇

Like a good number of American women of
the era, Mrs. Lincoln was opposed to women's suffrage. In 1871, she wrote to Mrs. John Dahlgren,
author of *Thoughts on Female Suffrage:* "I have
read with great pleasure your *spirituelle brochure,*
and can assure you of my entire sympathy in your
opposition to what are falsely called woman
rights. As if we women in America were not in the
fullest possession of every right. . . . I would rec-
ommend our strong-minded sisters to take a trip
to Savoy or Saxony, where I have seen women
hitched to the plough or harnessed with dogs,
drawing little carts through the streets.

"The movement seems to me, however, one of
those which should be treated with wholesome
neglect, since should Congress give them the privilege of voting—those who would avail themselves
of it are sure to behave in so inconsequent a
manner as to reduce the whole matter to an
absurdity."

⌇

As the Civil War dragged on, Mrs. Lincoln
wondered, "Will we ever awake from this hideous
nightmare?"

⌇

An ardent abolitionist who had nothing but
contempt for her four brothers and three broth-

ers-in-law who were Confederate soldiers, she nonetheless suffered outrageous smears. One such held that rebel spies came by ladder to her bedroom window, where she passed them military secrets. "I seem to be the scapegoat for both the North and the South!" she exclaimed.

✧

Some found Mrs. Lincoln pathologically self-centered. Others criticized her style of dress. "I want the women to mind their own business. I intend to wear what I please," she countered.

✧

"I do not belong to the public; my character is wholly domestic, and the public have nothing to do with it."

✧

"Oh it is no use to make any defense; all such efforts would only make me a target for new attacks."

✧

Later in life, Mrs. Lincoln reflected indirectly on what life had taught her: "You should go out every day and enjoy yourself. . . . Trouble comes soon enough . . . you must enjoy life, whenever you can . . . knowing full well by experience that power & high position do not ensure a bed of roses."

Eliza Johnson

b. 1810   d. 1876

First Lady
APRIL 15, 1865–MARCH 4, 1869

Seventeen-year-old Eliza McCardle Johnson took it upon herself to share her basic education with her eighteen-year-old husband, Andrew Johnson, a tailor who knew his letters but could neither write nor do arithmetic when they met. She is reported to have known that the two would fall in love from the moment she saw him. Their marriage was happiest before the onset of the Civil War. Mr. Johnson fought for the Union, like most other Eastern Tennesseeans. During the war years, Mrs. Johnson had to endure many trials on the home front. Confederate forces once raided her home while she was there, and she also suffered the pain of losing her son and a son-in-law in the conflict.

Poor health had turned Mrs. Johnson into an invalid by the time the war ended, and she could not fully attend to or enjoy the social duties of the First Lady during her time in the White House. She looked after her extended family's affairs but depended on her oldest daughter, Martha Patterson, to act as hostess for most public occasions. During President Johnson's impeachment trial, his wife insisted that all White House entertaining would continue without pause. She maintained that her husband was not at fault. After hearing Congress's verdict, she said, "I knew he'd be acquitted; I knew it." Mrs. Johnson died in 1876, six months after her husband's death.

That Eliza Johnson is one of the least-known First Ladies of them all could be explained by the following quotation—one of the few: "It's all very well for those who like it, but I do not like this public life at all. I often wish the time would come when we could return to where I feel we best belong."

◌

It became folklore that when she first saw her future husband she said, "There goes my beau!"

◌

After the grievous assassination of Abraham Lincoln, Mrs. Johnson told some White House guests, "We are plain people from the mountains of Tennessee, called here for a short time by a calamity. I trust too much will not be expected of us."

Julia Grant

b. 1826   d. 1902

First Lady
MARCH 4, 1869–MARCH 4, 1877

*J*ulia Boggs Dent Grant, daughter of
a St. Louis plantation owner, fell in love
with Lieutenant Ulysses S. Grant, but the
two had to wait out the four years of the Mexican
War to be married. Mrs. Grant often went with her
husband to lonely army outposts, and during the
Civil War she traveled to be with him whenever

possible. After the war hero was elected to the presidency in 1869, Mrs. Grant began an extravagant pattern of social entertainment and dressed at the height of fashion. Her daughter Nellie was married in the White House. At the end of their eight-year term as first family, General and Mrs. Grant toured Europe and were greeted with honors and riches wherever they went.

After leaving office, Mr. Grant lost all of the family's money in a failed business venture. In order to provide income for his wife, he hurriedly wrote his memoirs to assure their completion before he died of cancer. Mrs. Grant was able to live the rest of her life in financial comfort with the money from the book's sales. When Grant's Tomb was dedicated in 1897, Mrs. Grant eulogized, "The light of his glorious fame still reaches out to me, falls upon me, and warms me." She was buried next to her husband in 1902.

"I had enjoyed my independence too long to submit quietly."

Recalling the assassination of President Lincoln, Mrs. Grant said, "The whole land . . . now filled with . . . woe."

Mrs. Grant was intensely gratified by her eight-year tenure as First Lady. "My life at the White House," she told a later interviewer, "was like a bright and beautiful dream, and we were immeasurably happy. It was quite the happiest period of my life. . . . I am a woman and the life at the White House was a garden spot of orchids, and I wish it might have continued forever, except that it would have deterred others from enjoying the same privilege."

༂

She wrote to her son: "The fact is . . . the only way now to get along is to take the world as you find it and make the best of it. It will be the means of satisfying your feelings much better than by *showing* them your dislike. . . . That is the way to *triumph* and to make your enemies even speak well of you."

༂

When the time came to leave the White House, with no home to return to (they had sold their small house in Galena, Illinois), Mrs. Grant actually broke into tears: "Oh, Ulys," she told her husband, "I feel like a waif."

LUCY HAYES

b. 1831   d. 1889

First Lady
MARCH 4, 1877–MARCH 4, 1881

*L*ucy *Ware Webb Hayes* was a beloved and benevolent First Lady who became an idol to some as the herald of "the new woman era." Mrs. Hayes was well educated for a woman in the mid-nineteenth century, graduating from the Cincinnati, Ohio, Wesleyan Female College at the age of eighteen. After marrying Rutherford B. Hayes, she created a happy, devout home for her family. Her husband agreed with her religion-based opposition to slavery and supported the Union's efforts in the Civil War. Mrs. Hayes, called "Mother Lucy" by her husband's troops, assisted and comforted the battle-torn soldiers as much as she could during the conflict. Thereafter she maintained her humanitarian attitude toward politics as she advised her husband.

Mrs. Hayes served as a successful social coordinator and patron of good causes during her husband's terms as Governor of Ohio and as President. The temperance advocate never served alcohol at social functions and yet was one of the most popular hostesses at the White House. After Congress outlawed the annual children's egg-rolling event because it was ruining the grass on the Capitol grounds, Mrs. Hayes offered the White House lawn as a new location for the tradition. The Easter Monday activity has been held at the White House ever since. Mrs. Hayes spent eight happy years of retirement with her husband in Ohio until she died in 1889.

Though it wasn't until after her four years as First Lady that she received the nickname "Lemonade Lucy," Mrs. Hayes was most famous for her commitment to temperance. "I trust I am not a fanatic, but I do want my influence to be always in favor of temperance."

LUCRETIA GARFIELD

b. 1832   d. 1918

First Lady
MARCH 4, 1881–SEPTEMBER 19, 1881

*T*hough a member of the conservative Disciples of Christ and a reserved woman who did not wish for a public life, Lucretia "Crete" Rudolph Garfield understood how important social entertainment was to her husband's political success and filled that capacity with dignity and true hospitality. Mrs. Garfield was the

third consecutive First Lady to be married to a
former Civil War general who rose from humble
beginnings to the highest civic office. The
Garfields married in 1858 after a cautious and
extended courtship. However, throughout their
married life the couple grew ever closer, becoming almost inseparable by the time James A.
Garfield was elected president. The Garfields
especially enjoyed reading together and engaging
in intellectual discussions in their literary group.

Mrs. Garfield was stricken with malaria—and
probably nervous exhaustion as well—in May of
her first year as First Lady. Her husband was dis-
traught over her condition. While she was trying
to recuperate at a seaside resort, Mr. Garfield was
shot on July 2, 1881. The whole country admired
the poise and strength that the First Lady showed
during Mr. Garfield's eighty-day battle with the
wound. He died in September, and for the remaining thirty-six years of her life, Mrs. Garfield lived
privately in Ohio, collecting the records of her
husband's public life. She died in 1918.

Lucretia Garfield was fiercely independent, making her own living as a schoolteacher. Just prior to
the wedding, she wrote to Mr. Garfield: "My heart
is not yet schooled to an entire submission to that
destiny which will make the wife of one who mar-
ries me." Still, she kept promising "to try harder
than ever before to be the best little wife possible.
You need not be a bit afraid of my introducing

ever again one of those long talks that strike such a terror in you."

❧

Early in the summer during which Mr. Garfield received the presidential nomination, Mrs. Garfield wrote him: "I don't want you to have the nomination merely because no one else can get it, I want you to have it when the whole country calls for you. . . . My ambition does not fall short of that."

❧

Long before she became First Lady, Mrs. Garfield had been compelled to take on a variety of domestic chores that were not as appealing to her as cultural and literary affairs. Making huge batches of bread was one such chore, so she determined that she would overcome her dislike for the duty by taking a very special interest in it. She wrote: "The whole of life became brighter. The very sunshine seemed to be flowing down through my spirit into the white loaves, and now I believe my table is furnished with better bread than ever before; and this truth, as old as creation, seems just now to have become fully mine—that I need not be the shrinking slave of toil, but its regal master."

❧

She once told her husband, "Very many men may be loved devotedly by wives who know them to be worthless. But I think when a man has a

wife who holds him in large esteem . . . he has
reason to believe in his own worth."

***

On another occasion, she wanted to remind
her husband that equality was her right: "You
have been king of your work so long that maybe
you will laugh at me for having lived so long without my crown, but I am too glad to have found it
at all to be entirely disconcerted even by your
merriment. Now, I wonder if right here does not
lie that 'terrible wrong,' or at least some of it, of
which the woman suffragists complain. The
wrongly educated woman thinks her duties a dis-
grace, and frets under them or shirks them if she
can. She sees man triumphantly pursuing his
vocations, and thinks it is the kind of work he
does which makes him grand and regnant;
whereas it is not the kind of work at all, but the
way in which and the spirit with which he does
it."

***

"It is horrible to be a man, but the grinding
misery of being a woman between the upper and
nether millstone of household cares and training
children is almost as bad. To be half civilized with
some aspirations for enlightenment and obliged
to spend the largest part of the time the victim
of young barbarians keeps one in perpetual
ferment."

FRANCES CLEVELAND

b. 1864   d. 1947

First Lady
JUNE 2, 1886–MARCH 4, 1889;
MARCH 4, 1893–MARCH 4, 1897

The relationship between Frances
Folsom Cleveland and Grover Cleveland
was unusual, to say the least. As her
father's law partner, the twenty-seven-year-old
man bought his future wife her first baby car-
riage. After her father died, Mr. Cleveland was

never her legal guardian, but he was the administrator of her estate and her trusted advisor. The two began to exchange letters while "Frank" was at Wells College. While Mr. Cleveland was in office, the couple's fondness for each other blossomed into love, and they married in 1886.

The first woman to marry a President in the White House took over the duties of First Lady from President Cleveland's sister, Rose Elizabeth Cleveland. The new Mrs. Cleveland charmed society with her remarkable beauty and charm. To accommodate working women's schedules, she held special Saturday-afternoon receptions. She gave birth to her second and third daughters during Mr. Cleveland's second term. Mrs. Cleveland survived her first husband and married a Princeton professor. She lived to be eighty-three years old.

When Mr. Cleveland failed to win his bid for reelection, the indignant Mrs. Cleveland told the White House servants upon her departure, "I want you to take good care of the house. . . . We are coming back in just four years."

And sure enough, they did.

CAROLINE HARRISON

b. 1832   d. 1892

First Lady
MARCH 4, 1889–OCTOBER 25, 1892

un-loving Caroline Lavinia Scott Harrison married the reserved young Benjamin Harrison in 1853. He became a general in the Civil War while she raised their two children and contributed her time to charities and church activities. She enjoyed dancing and allowed her daughter to take lessons despite the views of her church. Mrs. Harrison also was a talented pianist and a good amateur painter.

During her time as First Lady, Mrs. Harrison managed to have the White House renovated to help accommodate her extended family that lived in the mansion. She began the White House china collection and worked for many charities. She helped raise money for Johns Hopkins University with the stipulation that it begin to admit women. She died in the White House in 1892 of tuberculosis. Her daughter served as hostess for the rest of her father's term.

When her husband became President in 1889, Caroline Harrison told reporters, "I am very anxious to see the family of the President provided for properly, and while I am here I hope to get the present building put into good condition."

"We have within ourselves the only element of destruction; our foes are from within, not without. It has been said 'that the men to make a country are made by self-denial,' and is it not true, that the society to live and grow and become what we desire it to be, must be composed of self-denying women? Since this society has been organized and so much thought and reading directed to the early struggles of this country, it has been made plain that much of its success was due to . . . women of that era. The unselfish part they acted constantly commands itself to our admiration and example. If there is no abatement in this element of success in our ranks, I feel sure that their daughters can perpetuate a society worthy the cause and worthy themselves."

IDA MCKINLEY

b. 1847   d. 1907

First Lady
MARCH 4, 1897–SEPTEMBER 14, 1901

da Saxton McKinley was a beautiful socialite from Canton, Ohio, when she married Major William McKinley. She was well educated and had traveled abroad. She met her future husband while working in her father's bank as a cashier, and after they married they lived a happy, family-centered life. But soon after the

birth of her second daughter, she was afflicted
with epilepsy and phlebitis. Her daughters died at
a young age.

Mrs. McKinley had been an invalid for twenty-
four years by the time she became First Lady in
1897. The First Family, their guests, and the press
were very discreet about her chronic illness, and
their efforts to act as if nothing was wrong were
so successful that her health problems did not
come to light until recently. Mr. McKinley was
utterly devoted to his wife and took great pains to
ensure that she was near his side at all times so
that he could care for her if she had a seizure. At
formal receptions, Mrs. McKinley would welcome
guests seated in a chair, holding a flower bouquet
so that no one would shake her hand. After Mr.
McKinley was shot in 1901, his thoughts centered
on the fragile First Lady: "My wife—be careful,
Cortelyou, how you tell her—oh, be careful," he
said to his secretary. Mrs. McKinley visited her
husband's grave almost daily for the remaining six
years of her life until her death in 1907.

In one of her few letters extant, Ida McKinley
wrote to an old friend about life after her husband's death: "I am more lonely every day I live."

EDITH ROOSEVELT

b. 1861   d. 1948

First Lady
SEPTEMBER 14, 1901–MARCH 4, 1909

*E*dith *Kermit Carow Roosevelt* was a childhood friend of her future husband Theodore, whom she called "Teedie." As she grew up and went to finishing school, she often accompanied the young Roosevelt on summer outings until they broke off contact when he began attending Harvard. She attended his first wedding, but they lived separate lives for years, until he became a widower with an infant daughter. They married in 1886. They had five children, and one of the active Mrs. Roosevelt's young sons once said, "When Mother was a little girl, she must have been a boy!"

After the Roosevelts moved into the White House, Mrs. Roosevelt's social training served her well as she supervised arrangements for the marriage of her husband's first child and the debut of her daughter Ethel. An aide described Mrs. Roosevelt as "always the gentle, high-bred hostess; smiling often at what went on around her, yet never critical of the ignorant and tolerant always of the little insincerities of political life." Mrs. Roosevelt's down-to-earth demeanor balanced the president's outgoing personality. He wrote to Theodore Jr., "If Mother had been a mere unhealthy Patient Griselda I might have grown set in selfish and inconsiderate ways." After her husband's death, Edith Roosevelt enjoyed reading and participated in volunteer work until she died at the age of eighty-seven in 1948.

"A lady's name should appear in print only three times: at her birth, marriage, and death."

"One hates to feel that all one's life is public property."

HELEN TAFT

b. 1861   d. 1943

First Lady
MARCH 4, 1909–MARCH 4, 1913

Helen Herron Taft grew up studying music in Cincinnati, Ohio. The willful and intellectual young woman married William Howard Taft, a young lawyer, in 1886. He suggested to his wife, whom he described as "self-contained, independent, and of unusual application," that they might reach the nation's capital—

when she became Secretary of the Treasury!
Though a political life was out of reach for her, as
for all women of her day, Mrs. Taft supported her
husband as he moved up the judicial ladder. She
moved her whole family to the war-torn Philippines
when he became head of American civil government there in 1900 and later enjoyed traveling
with him while he was Secretary of War.

In 1909, after only two months as First Lady,
Mrs. Taft had a severe stroke. However, she battled back within a year to again create a thriving
social scene at the White House. Her daughter
Helen debuted during this time. Mrs. Taft chroni-
cled her time as First Lady in a book, *Recollections
of Full Years*. She died in 1943.

Mrs. Taft wanted her husband to become President so badly that she spent night and day in nervous political maneuverings. "The ups and downs
of such a campaign, the prophecies, the hopes, the
fears aroused by favorable and opposing newspapers were all new and trying to me, and in a way I
think I was under as great a nervous strain as my
husband was."

When Mrs. Taft became First Lady, she wanted
to make sure people noticed her. After her husband's inauguration at the Capitol, she rode back
with him to the White House. Customarily the
place alongside the new President in this proces-

sion was reserved for the outgoing chief executive or some other male dignitary. "Of course there were objections," she later wrote, "but I had my way and in spite of protests took my place at my husband's side."

⌇

A White House first: Mrs. Taft had uniformed servants stationed at the front door to receive visitors and to offer instructions to sightseers. She commented, "Many a time I have seen strangers wander up to the door looking in vain for someone to whom it seemed right and proper to address a question or hand a visiting card," and she thought "many a timid visitor has had reason to be thankful for the change."

⌇

Mrs. Taft hired a housekeeper, Elizabeth Jaffray, to oversee purchasing and staff, because, she explained, "I wanted a woman who could relieve me of the supervision of such details as no man, expert steward though he might be, would ever recognize."

⌇

Helen Taft became one of those few First Ladies who was a kind of "co-President." She herself admitted, "I had always had the satisfaction of knowing almost as much as he about the politics and intricacies of any situation in which he found himself, and my life was filled with interests of a most unusual kind."

❧

When asked who had first thought of Mr. Taft running for President, she replied succinctly, "I did!"

❧

"I believe in the best and most thorough education for everyone, men and women," Mrs. Taft stated. "My idea about higher culture for women is that it makes them great in intellect and soul, develops the lofty conception of womanhood; not that it makes them a poor imitation of a man . . . woman is the complement of man. . . . No fundamental superiority or inferiority between the two appears plain to me. The only superiority lies in the way in which the responsibilities of life are discharged. Viewed in this light, some wives are superior to their husbands, some . . . women to men in varying circumstances. Education for women, as much as is obtainable, possesses to my mind, far greater advantages than the commercial one of providing means for making a livelihood. This is a very great benefit, when necessary."

❧

"I do not believe in a woman meddling in politics or asserting herself along those lines, but I think any woman can discuss with her husband topics of national interest and, in many instances, she might give her opinion of questions with which, through study and contact, she has become familiar. . . . Mr. Taft always held his conferences at our home, and, naturally, I heard these matters discussed more freely."

꒰

Obviously, a debilitating stroke affected such a powerful woman with tremendous force. Left unable to speak, she scribbled a note to her husband: "I do not like this thing of being silent, but I don't know what to do about it."

꒰

On April 16, 1912, when the White Star Line wired the President his requested list of those who had survived the sinking of the *Titanic*, one of their closest friend's names was not there. A gentleman to the bitter end, when he was told that the *Titanic* was sinking into the North Atlantic, the man changed into white tie and waited to die. Mrs. Taft wrote of "our close and dearly loved friend" that he drowned "facing death like a soldier, after the lives of nearly all the women and children had been saved." She added, "we felt that he belonged to us . . . nothing in all our experience ever touched us as deeply as the tragedy of his death."

ELLEN WILSON

b. 1860   d. 1914

First Lady
MARCH 4, 1913–AUGUST 6, 1914

Thomas "Tommy" Woodrow Wilson fell in love with the beautiful and sweet Southern belle Ellen Louise Axson Wilson while he was visiting her home in Rome, Georgia. They married in 1885, and over the course of their thirty-year marriage they gave each other over 1,400 love notes. Soon after the wedding, Mr.

Wilson took a teaching job at Bryn Mawr College
in Pennsylvania. Mrs. Wilson insisted that her
children not be born Yankees, so she traveled
back home to have her first two children. Her
third was born in Connecticut (Mr. Wilson was
teaching at Wesleyan then). After her husband
took a high-profile position at Princeton University,
Ellen Wilson often escaped the stress of those
social duties by painting. Her work compares
favorably with that of professional artists of the
period. After moving into the White House as First
Lady in 1913, Mrs. Wilson had a skylight installed
to create a studio in which to work.

Mrs. Wilson's simple style of entertaining was
pleasant, and the Wilsons opted not to have an
inaugural ball. But Mrs. Wilson was ambitious in
her social reform projects. She visited alleys and
slums to increase awareness of the living conditions of poor African Americans. She worked to
pass a slum clearance bill through Congress.
Unfortunately, it took her death, in 1914 of
Bright's disease, to push the bill through.

She once said, "I am naturally the most unambi-
tious of women and life in the White House has no
attractions for me."

Discussing her tenure as First Lady, Ellen
Wilson said, "A person would be a fool who lets
his head be turned by externals; they simply go
with the position."

EDITH WILSON

b. 1872   d. 1961

First Lady
DECEMBER 18, 1915–MARCH 4, 1921

*E*dith Bolling Galt Wilson met
Woodrow Wilson when she was a widow
and he was mourning the loss of his first
wife. He proposed in 1915, saying, "in this place
time is not measured by weeks, or months, or
years, but by deep human experiences." In 1919,
while working for Senate approval of the League

of Nations Convenant, President Wilson suffered a paralyzing stroke. The First Lady took over many of his duties, earning her the titles "Secret President" and "First Woman to Run the Government." She made no policy decisions, preferring instead to pass them along to her husband's staff. Mrs. Wilson outlived her husband by thirty-seven years, dying on the anniversary of his birth, December 28, in 1961.

"Much as I enjoy your delicious love letters," the widowed woman wrote the widowed President during their courtship, "I enjoy even more the ones in which you tell me . . . of what you are working on."

In October 1919, President Wilson was paralyzed by a stroke. For the ensuing eighteen months, Edith Wilson took charge of the White House—and, it is widely believed, of the executive branch of the government. In her memoirs, she defended her actions:

> Once my husband was out of immediate danger, the burning question was how Mr. Wilson might best serve the country, preserve his own life, and if possible recover. Many people, among them some I had counted as friends, have written of my overwhelming ambition to act as President; of my exclusion

of all advice, and so forth. I am trying here to write as though I had taken the oath to tell the truth, the whole truth, and nothing but the truth—so help me God.

I asked the doctors to be frank with me; that I must know what the outcome would probably be, so as to be honest with the people. They all said that as the brain was as clear as ever, with the progress made in the past few days, there was every reason to think recovery possible. . . . But recovery could not be hoped for, they said, unless the President were released from every disturbing problem during these days of Nature's effort to repair the damage done.

"How can that be," I asked the doctors, "when everything that comes to an executive is a problem? How can I protect him from problems when the country looks to the President as the leader?"

Dr. Dercum leaned toward me and said: "Madam, it is a grave situation, but I think you can solve it. Have everything come to you; weight the importance of each matter, and see if it is possible by consultations with the respective heads of the departments to solve them without the guidance of your husband. In this way you can save him a great deal. But always keep in mind that every time you take him a new anxiety or problem to excite him, you are turning a knife in an open wound." . . .

"Then," I said, "had he better not resign, let Mr. Marshall succeed to the Presidency and he himself get that complete rest that is so vital to his life?"

"No," the doctor said, "not if you feel equal to what I suggested. For Mr. Wilson to resign would have a bad effect on the country, and a serious effect on our patient. He has staked his life and made his promise to the world to do all in his power to get the Treaty ratified and make the League of Nations complete. If he resigns, the greatest incentive to recovery is gone; and as his mind is clear as crystal he can still do more with even a maimed body than anyone else. He has the utmost confidence in you. Dr. Grayson tells me that he has always discussed public affairs with you; so you will not come to them uninformed."

So began my stewardship. I studied every paper, sent from the different Secretaries or Senators, and tried to digest and present in tabloid form the things that, despite my vigilance, had to go to the President. I myself never made a single decision regarding the disposition of public affairs. The only decision that was mine was what was important and what was not, and the *very* important decision of when to present matters to my husband."

✌

Commenting on the period following her husband's stroke, Edith Wilson noted, "Of course the burning question was how best to serve the country—and yet protect the President."

Florence Harding

b. 1860   d. 1924

First Lady
MARCH 4, 1921–AUGUST 3, 1923

lorence Kling De Wolfe Harding
grew up in Marion, Ohio, where she became
strong-willed and resourceful under her
entrepreneurial father's influence. She studied
music in the Cincinnati Conservatory, but at age
nineteen she eloped with a neighbor. The man
soon deserted her, leaving her with a baby son.

Proud and self-reliant, she got a divorce, supporting herself and her child by giving piano lessons,
and later by running the Marion newspaper's circu-
lation department. A friend said, "No pennies
escaped her."

After Warren G. Harding bought Marion's
newspaper, they soon married. As Mr. Harding
rose through the ranks of civil service, Mrs.
Harding worked tirelessly in his election
campaigns.

When she became First Lady, Florence
Harding continued her active lifestyle despite a
chronic kidney ailment. She entertained extensively—even serving alcohol illegally during
White House poker games. Mrs. Harding enjoyed
traveling with her husband and was with President Harding in California when he died in 1923.
Devastated by the loss, she died the next year.

The powerful and assertive Mrs. Harding's first
gesture as First Lady was to reopen the White
House gates to the public. The gates had been
locked and carefully guarded ever since the war
years and President Wilson's illness. Mrs. Harding
even pulled up the window shades so the swarms
of people moving over the grounds could get a
look inside. "It's their White House," she said. "Let
them look in if they want to."

"Well, Warren," she told her husband in 1921, "I have got you the Presidency; what are you going to do with it?"

∽

She said of herself, "I have only one real hobby—my husband."

∽

"I know what's best for the President," she often insisted. "I put him in the White House. He does well when he listens to me and poorly when he does not."

∽

Mrs. Harding knew there were limits to how far she could go before prompting criticism. In one letter, which she decided against sending, she wrote, "If the career is the husband's, the wife can merge her own with it, if it is to be the wife's as it undoubtedly will be in an increasing proportion of cases, then the husband may, with no sacrifice of self-respect or of recognition . . . permit himself to be the less prominent and distinguished member of the combination."

GRACE COOLIDGE

b. 1879   d. 1957

First Lady
AUGUST 3, 1923–MARCH 4, 1929

race Anna Goodhue Coolidge worked
at the Clarke School for the Deaf before she
married Calvin Coolidge in 1905. The couple lived in half of a duplex, scrimping and saving
in order to keep up appearances while he strug-
gled as a small-town New England lawyer. Mrs.
Coolidge was the one who played catch with their

sons. She was also the one who worked to make influential acquaintances as Mr. Coolidge moved into the political arena. Her friendliness always served to balance out her husband's shyness, and their frugality (they lived in the duplex until Mr. Coolidge became Governor of Massachusetts) translated into simple yet decorous entertainment when they became the First Family in 1923.

Two years after she left the White House, Mrs. Coolidge was voted one of America's twelve greatest living women, and the National Institute of Social Sciences gave her a gold medal for "fine personal influence exerted as First Lady of the Land." She enjoyed life with her husband until his death in 1933. He said in his autobiography, "For almost a quarter of a century she has borne with my infirmities, and I have rejoiced in her graces." As a widow, Mrs. Coolidge traveled to Europe and flew on an airplane, both for the first time, continuing to relish life until her death in 1957.

Mrs. Coolidge gave of herself completely to the American public while serving as First Lady. The beloved hostess described the public role that she fulfilled: "When I reflect upon my Washington career I wonder how I ever faced it. . . . There was a sense of detachment. This was I, and yet not I— this was the wife of the President and she took precedence over me; my personal likes and dislikes must be subordinated to the consideration of those things which were required of her."

❧

Mrs. Coolidge's unmitigated joy at being in the White House was impossible to hide. She wrote to a group of friends: "I wish I could describe my varied sensations when we came in. . . . I wish I could tell you all that is in my heart—but there is so much that even I am bewildered. Alice in Wonderland or Babes in the Woods—however you wish to regard me."

❧

After becoming a national public figure, Mrs. Coolidge played down her former popularity. "When I can no longer speak for myself, I hope nobody will attempt to show that I was one of the most popular girls in the college. . . . I was not . . . but I had many unusual friends whose loyalty has stood the test of the years."

❧

"I had my hands full discharging the duties of the position to which I had not been elected," Mrs. Coolidge once complained.

❧

"Being wife to a government worker is a very confining position."

❧

"We New England women cling to the old way, and being the President's wife isn't going to make me think less about the domestic duties I've always loved."

✣

"Well, I thought I would get [Mr. Coolidge] to enjoy life and have fun, but he was not very easy to instruct in that way."

✣

Five years after the blood-poisoning death of her sixteen-year-old son, Calvin, Grace Coolidge composed a poem that was later read at her own funeral. It began:

> You my son
> Have shown me God.
> Your kiss upon my cheek
> Has made me feel the gentle touch
> Of Him who leads us on.

LOU HOOVER

b. 1874   d. 1944

First Lady

MARCH 4, 1929–MARCH 4, 1933

---

*L*ou *Henry Hoover* met her future
husband Herbert Hoover in a geology lab
while both were attending Stanford
University. Mrs. Hoover enjoyed hunting, camp-
ing, riding, and rock collecting during her early
teenage years in California. After she graduated
from Stanford with a geology and mining major,
the couple wed and traveled the globe as Mr.

Hoover made his fortune as a mining engineer. In 1921 Mr. Hoover was appointed Secretary of Commerce, and Mrs. Hoover entered the social circle of a cabinet member's wife. For a time she was the president of the Girl Scouts of America.

A Maine congressman once sent an aide to the Hoover White House bearing a very large fish as a present from the state of Maine, and Mrs. Hoover had it sent directly to the kitchen. Then the congressman arrived and revealed that he had sent the fish so that he could be photographed with it and the President. By the time Mrs. Hoover got to the kitchen, the fish had been decapitated. Doing some very quick thinking, she sent the fish and its head to Lillian Parks, the White House seamstress, who sewed the head back on. The photograph was taken, and nobody in Maine could have noticed anything amiss.

While in the White House, the Hoovers continued to entertain lavishly despite the onset of the Great Depression. They ate dinner alone only on their anniversary. When the cost of social events exceeded the social budget, they paid for the difference from their private fortune. Mrs. Hoover also used her own money to restore Lincoln's study and create a period sitting room by reproducing furniture owned by Monroe. Lou Hoover was a selflessly charitable woman. After her death in 1944, Mr. Hoover learned that she had helped pay for the education "of a multitude of boys and girls."

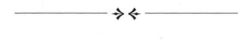

When she entered Stanford in 1894 to pursue studies in geology, practically everybody she knew asked her: who would marry a woman geologist? She always replied that she did not intend to give up her own interests if she did get married. "I want a man who loves the mountains, the rocks, and the oceans like my father does."

⌇

"I enjoy campaigning," she once said, "because my husband makes the speeches—and I receive the roses."

⌇

"It takes just as much courage to stick to the housework until it is done as it does to go out and meet a bear," Mrs. Hoover told a Girl Scout convention in 1927.

⌇

"It isn't so important what others think of you as what you feel inside."

ELEANOR ROOSEVELT

b. 1884 d. 1962

First Lady
MARCH 4, 1933–APRIL 12, 1945

The shy and awkward, yet incredibly intelligent and compassionate Anna Eleanor Roosevelt Roosevelt wrote at the age of fourteen: "No matter how plain a woman may be if truth and loyalty are stamped upon her face all will be attracted to her." She worked as a social worker before marrying her distant cousin

Franklin Delano Roosevelt in 1905. Her Uncle
Theodore, then the President, gave her away in
the wedding. She wrote regarding the early years
of the marriage, after she had given birth to six
children, "I suppose I was fitting pretty well into
the pattern of a fairly conventional, quiet, young
society matron." But then in 1918 Mrs. Roosevelt
found out that her husband was having an affair
with her social secretary. The couple later recon-
ciled, but Mrs. Roosevelt soon rejected the conventional path laid out for her and became much
more active, especially in the League of Women
Voters and the Women's Trade Union League.
After her husband was incapacitated by polio, she
joined the women's division of New York's State
Democratic Committee to help him maintain visi-
bility in the political arena.

During the twelve years of Mr. Roosevelt's
presidency, Mrs. Roosevelt broke precedent after
precedent in her role as First Lady. She held press
conferences, traveled, gave lectures, wrote books,
and wrote a syndicated daily newspaper editorial
column, "My Day," which allowed her a powerful
channel through which to effect social and political change in America. She supported the National Youth Administration's efforts to increase the
employment rate of young people.

Unhampered by the duties of political back-
scratching, she had the freedom to champion liberal causes, including the fight for racial equality.
After the Daughters of the American Revolution

refused to allow black singer Marian Anderson to sing in Constitution Hall, Mrs. Roosevelt resigned from the organization and arranged for Ms. Anderson to sing at the Lincoln Memorial on Easter Sunday. She supported the desegregation of the army and visited American soldiers the world over during World War II. After her husband's death, she founded Americans for Democratic Action and became the American spokesperson in the United Nations. During her eight years at the UN, she served as chairperson for the committee that drafted the Universal Declaration of Human Rights. Mrs. Roosevelt died in 1962.

Eleanor Roosevelt's parents were FDR's godparents, so she met her fifth cousin at their future home in Hyde Park at the age of two. She later wrote, "I am told that Franklin, probably under protest, crawled around the nursery (which has since been our children's), bearing me on his back."

"The basic thing which contributes to charm is the ability to forget oneself and be engrossed in other people."

"Work is almost the best way to pull oneself out of the depths."

"In all human relationships, and marriage is one of the most difficult, I think perhaps the important qualities for all individuals are unselfishness and flexibility. Tact can be a help also, and real love which occasionally carries you beyond interest in yourself is essential."

⁓

"The successful wife is many women: lover, housekeeper, mother . . . a listening ear, a sympathetic voice, a tender and comforting hand . . . a stimulant to cheerfulness, a gracious hostess, and frequently one who shares with her husband the task of earning the family livelihood. I often have thought that less is expected of the president of a great corporation than of an American wife."

⁓

"I learned a long while ago not to make judgments on what other people do."

⁓

"I have the memory of an elephant. I can forgive, but I cannot forget."

⁓

"[Franklin] might have been happier with a wife who was completely uncritical. That I was never able to be, and he had to find it in other people."

⁓

"It's better to light a candle than to curse the darkness."

༬

"The happy home will be the one in which the woman is not considering that her husband's success is measured by his salary."

༬

"All human beings have failures, all human beings have needs and temptations and stresses. Men and women who live together through long years get to know one another's failings, but they also come to know what is worthy of respect and admiration in those they live with and in themselves. If at the end one can say, 'This man used to the limit the powers that God granted him; he was worthy of love and respect and of the sacrifices of many people, made in order that he might achieve what he deemed to be his task, then that life has been lived well and there are no regrets.'"

༬

Although over one million African American men served their country during World War II, they had to eat, sleep, live, train, and fight in segregated units. Mrs. Roosevelt was one of the earliest advocates of desegregation in the armed forces. In the following letter, addressed directly to her husband, she strongly recommends a groundbreaking meeting of black leaders, such as NAACP Executive Secretary Walter White, former Urban League Industrial Secretary T. Arnold Hill, and Brotherhood of Sleeping Car Porters President

A. Philip Randolph, with Secretary of War Henry L.
Stimson.

I have just heard that no meeting was
ever held between colored leaders like
Walter White, Mr. Hill, and Mr. Randolph,
with the secretary of War and Navy on the
subject of how the colored people can participate in the services.

There is growing feeling amongst the
colored people, and they are creating a feeling among many white people. They feel they
should be allowed to participate in any training that is going on, in the aviation, army,
navy, and have opportunities for service.

I would suggest that a conference be
held with the attitude of the gentlemen:
these are our difficulties, how do you suggest
that we make a beginning to change the
situation?

There is no use of going into a conference unless they have the intention of doing
something. This is going to be very bad politically, besides being intrinsically wrong, and I
think you should ask that a meeting be held
and if you can not be present yourself, you
should ask them to give you a report and it
might be well to have General Watson
present.

E.R.

In 1945, Mrs. Roosevelt articulated the way that many American women felt, but couldn't express: "I think anything connected with the home is as much the husband's work as the wife's."

❧

"I think women are often superior to men in their intuition about people; in their executive ability when they are handling detailed work, and in their ability to subordinate themselves to a cause or to another individual if they think that is the way to serve a cause."

❧

"It is essential for a woman to develop her own interests . . . so as not to lose the possibility of being a stimulating personality."

❧

"Looks alone do not make one attractive. If you cultivate your mind and your spirit, you can have charm, which is far more important than looks."

❧

"If you will forget about yourself, whether or not you are making a good impression on people, what they think of you, and you will think about them instead, you won't be shy."

❧

"The most rewarding activity for any woman, young or old, is to meet the needs of those who are nearest and dearest to her. She will not meet these adequately, however, if she has no interests and occupations of her own, since it is important that young families should never have the feeling that the older members of the family are languishing for their constant companionship. This makes the time they spend together less enjoyable and makes a duty out of something which should be a pleasure."

⤳

"Unless we make of ourselves persons whom we like, with whom when occasion demands, we can live pleasantly in solitude, we are poorly equipped for social life in any community."

⤳

"To leave the world richer—that is the ultimate success."

⤳

"Both parties to a successful marriage have to do a good deal of adjusting, and as women are usually more adaptable, I should not be surprised if they did the adjusting a little more gracefully and successfully than men."

⤳

"I personally think that probably it would be wiser if [getting married] were made far more difficult. We are constantly agitating the question of whether there should be uniform divorce laws, but I think it would be more to the point to discuss the question of under what conditions and restrictions people should marry."

❧

"I don't think children owe their parents any gratitude. It is love, not obligation, that brings about warm and happy relations within families."

❧

"I think, at a child's birth, if a mother could ask a fairy godmother to endow it with the most useful gift, that gift should be curiosity."

❧

"Children somehow have a way of knowing when people try to appear to be something that they are not."

❧

"I certainly do believe in teaching children to believe in Santa Claus."

❧

"I think children will miss a great deal if they never read fairy stories. Children live in a world of fantasy and if we try to take that away from them too young, I think they are the poorer for it."

❧

"I believe very strongly that it is better to allow children too much freedom than too little."

❧

"One has no right, once one's children are grown and mature, to interfere with their decisions."

❧

"Children, rich and poor, are the wealth of a nation. Their hands and their heads, as they grow to maturity, are going to determine what happens in every country in the world."

❧

"I have always felt it was a pity that so many people sent their children to private schools, because they are then less likely to work for improved public schools. I believe that, for the good of the community, more of us should have children in public schools, so we can fight together for better schools."

❧

"I do not think that religion can properly be taught in public schools."

❧

"Real education is knowledge that is not acquired from books alone."

❧

"Often in my talks with college students, I have been struck by the fact that few of them seem to know what they are or what their potentials are, where they are going or how, what they ought to do about their lives. Certainly the person who does not know where he is going or how to get there is not the material out of which leaders are made."

❧

"I have lived more than sixty years and I have heard young people condemned many times. I think nearly every generation is better than the last, and I certainly admire the present one."

ॐ

"We obtain our education at home, at school, and, most important, from life itself. The learning process must go on as long as we live. Nothing alive can stand still. Life is interesting only as long as it is a process of growth; or, to put it another way, we can grow only as long as we are interested."

ॐ

"I am for birth control, particularly in places having severe problems of overpopulation and insufficient food."

ॐ

"We all create the person we become by our choices as we go through life. In a very real sense, by the time we are adult, we are the sum total of the choices we have made."

ॐ

"Adapting one's plans to the needs of others is what makes life worth living."

ॐ

"Skill depends on practice, for it is only with practice that one becomes good at anything."

ॐ

"I think a woman's obligation is always to her husband. But if she is a wise woman, she will make her children feel that they, too, have an obligation to their father. Then there will be no conflicts because they will be one family with mutual interests all of them respect."

⨾

President Harry Truman appointed Mrs. Roosevelt the U.S. representative to the nascent United Nations in 1945. The UN was instantaneously perceived as a quarrelsome organization where complaints wasted the time of all involved. When the Korean War broke out, the notion of world peace seemed particularly impossible to achieve. Mrs. Roosevelt had always supported the establishment of the UN, and because the organization's image was so unfairly tarnished, she toured America extolling its importance in the world.

In 1953, she offered the following defense of the UN to the Illinois Congress of Parents and Teachers:

You have heard, as many of us have heard, the current saying "What good has come from the United Nations? Hasn't the United Nations failed? It was set up to bring us peace, and we don't have peace." But that is really a most unfortunate misconception. The object that the sovereign states hoped for when they wrote the charter in San Francisco was that we could use this machinery as united nations to achieve a peaceful world. But it's only machinery, and machinery doesn't work by itself. It's the people who make it work.

We have also heard it said that the United Nations is just a debating society, that it never accomplishes anything. Yet we have found over the years that it requires a good deal of talk for people to learn to understand one another. Even in the Congress of the United States we don't always find an immediate meeting of minds. Well, you take sixty sovereign nations, all religions, frequently different legal systems. How can you expect them immediately—within six or seven years, that is—to arrive at a meeting of minds? True, the breach has widened between us and the Soviets, but that breach might have broadened into a war if there hadn't been a place where we had to meet and where we were able to talk.

And if the United Nations is a debating society, do you feel that you have learned all you should about what conditions are all over the world—for instance, in India? I am sure that many of you have no conception of what it is to live in a country where there is always a famine somewhere. I know it wasn't until I went to India and saw the famine districts that I realized what it would be like if some part of my own country was always living under famine conditions. I know of no way in which we can learn these things as quickly as we are learning them from the information that comes to us through channels provided by the United Nations.

I get a lot of letters from people who say, "How can you expect the United Nations to succeed when you do not recognize God in the United Nations?" We have in the U.N. building a little room known as a prayer room to serve all devout people. From those who live according to their own religious standards I have learned a tremendous amount. I have learned to respect them, for I sometimes think that the same spirit pervades the good people in all religions. If you want others to respect your beliefs, you must in return give respect for theirs.

These are some of the things that you learn as you find yourself in close association with people from different parts of the world. It is because they are things that we all need to learn that I believe parents and teachers today have such a tremendous responsibility. They have to prepare our children for living as leaders in a world that will follow their leadership, if the world can respect it. And that will require of our children a greater knowledge of the rest of the world than any of us have ever had before. They are going to be leaders in a world where not only are there different religions and habits and customs but different races—and two-thirds of that world is made up of peoples of different colors.

When all is said and done, then, what we need is to know more about the United Nations and its action groups—the specialized agencies—if only because this is machinery that we people of the different nations must use. For if we do not know about it and if we do not back it up, it isn't going to be used as well as it might be. Furthermore, I feel very strongly that with more knowledge, many of the fears we have had about the United Nations will be dispelled.

Remember, this cooperation is so new, so new in every field, that it's very hard for any of us to work together even on what we think are simple things. So we shouldn't be discouraged when we do not achieve peace all at once. Peace is not going to drop on us from heaven. It is going to have to be worked for, with the hearts and minds and wills of human beings. I believe it can be achieved, but we are going to have to work much harder. We must strengthen it, at the same time learning about the rest of the world.

This is why parents and teachers today must have courage enough to stand up against waves of public opinion. At present we are going through a period of what I call unreasonable fears, fears that cause great suspicion among us. Many people are afraid to say what they think because it might by chance be something that somebody else might think subversive. Yet our nation has been built on differences of opinion, stated openly. Throughout our history we have had quite a number of people who stood for almost revolutionary ideas. But we have weathered the years, and we have come to be the leading nation of the world. And now it is a question of how well we prepare the next generation to take the burden from their elders. These young people have to know much more than we knew. We had to know about our own country; they have to know about the world. They have to feel and understand things that we didn't have to feel and understand at all.

We have to have unity. We have to believe in each other. We cannot be suspicious of everybody. Surely there are people among us who perhaps do not believe in the things that we think essential, but I think the vast majority of us are well rooted in the beliefs of freedom.

I think we can stand up against any infiltration or propaganda, but first we must have a feeling of confidence. We must really care

about bringing to the people of the world a
leadership that is good, a leadership that is
strong. I do not mean strong just in a military
and economic way but in a spiritual and
moral way. If we do have that feeling and can
impart it to our young people, I believe we
can do this job, the biggest job any nation has
ever had. We are at the crossroads. It is up to
us whether we move forward—slowly, to be
sure, but step by step—to a better world or
whether we fail.

What is going to happen? I do not know.
If we succeed, it will be because you and I, as
individuals, believe in ourselves and in the
need to work with our neighbors throughout
the world. I think we will hand on to our
children a struggle, but a struggle that will
give our nation the capacity to lead the
world toward peace and righteousness and
freedom.

ॐ

By 1961, relative to most female public figures,
Mrs. Roosevelt's feminism was downright outspoken: "With the modern gadgets we have in our
homes, almost every woman can do something
outside her home, and I think this is good. As a
rule, it gives a woman some interest that occupies
her mind, and so her outlook is fresher and more
abreast with her husband's. When he returns from
activities outside his home, he should have some-

one with something besides the daily routine of housework and child care to talk about."

✥

"No one is happy without the necessities and decencies of life . . . but I don't believe happiness is primarily a question of being either rich or poor."

✥

"Happiness is not a goal, it is a by-product."

✥

"Planning the budget and allotting the income should, I think, be a unifying force in the family, a matter in group discussion and decision."

✥

"A mature person is one who does not think only in absolutes, who is able to be objective even when deeply stirred emotionally, who has learned that there is both good and bad in all people and in all things, and who walks humbly and deals charitably with the circumstances of life, knowing that in this world no one is all-knowing and there-fore all of us need both love and charity."

✥

"I was for the experiment to do away by law with the drinking of hard liquor in this country, until I found we were becoming a nation of law-breakers. I decided then we could not legislate morals, and it was better not to have a law when so many good people broke it, but to trust to people to live up to their own standards and values."

☞

"Once your children are grown up and have children of their own, the problems are theirs, and the less the older generation interferes the better."

☞

"What one has to do usually can be done."

☞

"When you know that there is much to be done you are always looking forward instead of backward."

☞

"Only those who love really live, in spite of the pain it so often brings."

☞

"Curiously enough, I never minded criticism much. I think I learned very young that everything passes and if you just live it through, it comes to an end. If there is criticism and there is a foundation of right in it, well then it's criticism and you have to take it. If there is no foundation in it, sooner or later people are going to find out and in the meantime, it doesn't really matter much. The one thing I would mind would be if it really affected the people I loved—people whose feeling of affection it really disturbed."

꩜

"Age is a matter of mind as well as of the body. I have known people old in years who were yet young in their outlook on life and in some ways managed even to keep their bodies young by their mental processes."

꩜

"I doubt that anyone does not really believe in God. People may think they don't have any belief, but you will usually find that somewhere down in a human being's soul there is a belief in something beyond himself. In any case, I would not judge a man's character by his belief or his unbelief. I would judge his character by his deeds; and no matter what he said about his beliefs, his behavior would soon show whether he was a man of good character or bad."

꩜

When FDR died suddenly in Warm Springs, Georgia, Mrs. Roosevelt cabled her sons: "He did his job to the end as he would want you to do."

She then sent for Vice President Harry Truman, who did not know why he was being summoned to the White House with such urgency. He was shown into Mrs. Roosevelt's sitting room. She came forward, put a hand on his shoulder, and quietly said, "Harry, the President is dead."

Mr. Truman was speechless. Finally, he asked, "Is there anything I can do for you?" He later wrote that he would never forget her reply:

"Is there anything *we* can do for *you?*" she asked. "For you are the one in trouble now."

Harry Truman began his term as President just as the United States was poised to make the final push against Hitler in World War II. Soon after, Truman was faced with the historic decision to drop the atomic bombs on Japan.

～

"We have to accept what is in store for us, so why worry about it?"

～

"I wonder if one of the penalties of growing older is that you become more and more conscious that nothing in life is very permanent."

～

"Death is unnatural when it comes to the young, but with age it is normal and inevitable and, like everything else that has been inevitable in life, becomes easier to accept."

～

"It always seemed to me that there must be some kind of immortality, because it would be such a wasteful performance otherwise."

BESS TRUMAN

b. 1885   d. 1982

First Lady
APRIL 12, 1945–JANUARY 20, 1952

When *Elizabeth Virginia "Bess" Wallace Truman* returned to her hometown of Independence, Missouri, in 1952 after her time as First Lady, her friends and neighbors noted that she remained as unpretentious as she was before she accompanied her husband to Washington. But even though Bess

Truman referred to herself as a "nobody," her husband and childhood sweetheart Harry S Truman said that she was "a full partner in all my transactions" and introduced her as "the boss" while the couple was on the campaign trail.

Mrs. Truman did not enjoy living a public life, first as the Vice President's wife and then for almost eight years as First Lady. Her husband remarked that she was "not especially interested" in the "formalities and pomp of the artificiality which, as we had learned . . . inevitably surround the family of the President." Bess Truman fulfilled all of her social duties, but she preferred to remain a silent partner in the First Family—a drastic change from her predecessor, Eleanor Roosevelt. During President Truman's second term in office, the Trumans left the White House while the dilapidated building underwent major repairs. After leaving the capital for good, Mrs. Truman lived in Independence until her death in 1982. She lived to be ninety-seven years old—the longest life span of any First Lady.

Mrs. Truman was as no-nonsense as her husband. She maintained, "I couldn't possibly be anything like [Eleanor Roosevelt]. I wasn't going down in any mines."

When the press solicited interviews with her, Mrs. Truman wouldn't budge. When asked by the press what she was planning to wear on any particular occasion, she would snap, "It's none of their damned business."

❦

"You don't need to know me. I'm only the President's wife and the mother of his daughter."

❦

"I am not the one elected," she once stated. "I have nothing to say to the public."

❦

"I don't know what I'm going to do," she confided to a friend. "I'm not used to this awful public life." To another friend, she admitted that she was unhappy "to be where we are but there's nothing to be done about it except to do our best and forget about the sacrifices and many unpleasant things that bob up."

❦

It was noted that her only similarity to the towering presence of her predecessor in the White House was that both she and Mrs. Roosevelt had quite messy closets. "Well," Mrs. Truman said, "I'm pleased that I resemble Mrs. Roosevelt in at least one respect."

❦

Once, Mr. Truman found his wife casually burning in a fireplace some of the letters he had written to her. "Bess, you oughtn't to do that," he protested.

"Why not? I've read them several times," she replied.

"But think of history!" the President beseeched his wife.

"I have," muttered Mrs. Truman as she tossed the last of them into the fire.

✌

Mrs. Truman once attended a Grange meeting at Independence, Missouri, with a friend whose husband was making a speech about soil conservation. He ended his lecture by telling the gathered farmers, "Now remember—what you need is manure, manure—and more manure."

Mrs. Truman's friend was embarrassed and whispered to her, "Oh, dear, I've been trying to get him to say 'fertilizer.'"

Mrs. Truman whispered back, "And I've been trying to get Harry to say 'manure'!"

✌

Mrs. Truman defended her husband's decision to drop the atomic bomb on Hiroshima and Nagasaki: "Harry always placed high value on the life of a single American boy. If the war with Japan had been allowed to continue, it would have claimed the lives of perhaps a quarter-million American soldiers, and twice that number would have been maimed for life. It's difficult to calculate the number of Japanese lives that would have been lost . . . as many or more, undoubtedly, as died at Hiroshima and Nagasaki. So the atom bomb was the lesser weapon, although it's hard to look at it that way."

☙

"A woman's place in public is to sit beside her husband, be silent, and be sure her hat is on straight."

MAMIE EISENHOWER

b. 1896   d. 1979

First Lady
JANUARY 20, 1953–JANUARY 20, 1961

Marie "Mamie" Geneva Doud Eisenhower met her future husband Dwight D. Eisenhower in 1915 while he was on his first tour of duty at Fort Sam Houston and she was wintering in San Antonio, Texas. After they married, Mrs. Eisenhower accompanied her husband as he traveled from army post to army post the world over while he climbed the military ranks. She once estimated that she had moved twenty-seven times over the course of thirty-seven years.

Mrs. Eisenhower welcomed the opportunity to serve as First Lady in 1953. She enjoyed showing off her husband, whom she had so faithfully supported over the years. Her beauty and enthusiasm endeared her to the American people. The ease of air travel and increased awareness of the importance of foreign policy meant that Mrs. Eisenhower entertained an unprecedented number of world leaders. After two terms in office, the Eisenhowers moved to Gettysburg, Pennsylvania, to the first and only home that they ever owned. Mrs. Eisenhower died in 1979.

"Ike runs the country, and I turn the lamb chops."

"Every woman over fifty should stay in bed until noon."

"I never knew what a woman would want to be liberated from."

Mrs. Eisenhower's personal maid, Rose Woods, overheard her on the phone to a friend a week or so after she and Dwight arrived at the White House. "And I've just had the first good night's sleep I've had since we've been in the White House," she said. "Our new bed finally got here, and now I can reach over and pat Ike on his old bald head any time I want to!"

⌐⌐

Writing for *Today's Woman* magazine, Mrs. Eisenhower revealed her idea of feminism: "Let's face it. Our lives revolve around our men, and that is the way it should be. What real satisfaction is there without them? Being a wife is the best career that life has to offer a woman, but . . . it takes wit and straight thinking. . . . I can speak as strongly as I like about the dreadful mistakes . . . I was a spoiled brat when I married."

She addressed the question of women's professional careers: "Your husband is the boss—and don't forget it. I am very sorry for the young wife who . . . has in the back of her head the idea, I can always get a divorce, or who thinks, There is no future in all of this housework—I'll get a job. . . . The endless routine of a house sometimes seems like a meager, futile little job—especially when your husband comes home full of important news. . . . Those are the moments when a job that will take you out among people and give you extra money seems very desirable. But life will be far more rewarding if you do not yield to that temptation. If you do, you may find yourself with nothing but a job twenty years from now." And yet, paradoxically, she added, "Your independence . . . depend[s] on you," warning that the only way "to avoid debt . . . is for the husband to give his wife the paycheck and let her be responsible for it. . . . If he sets up charge accounts and pays the bills . . . things are almost certain to get out of hand."

✦

Rumors of Mr. Eisenhower's affair with Kay Summersby were rampant, but Mrs. Eisenhower pooh-poohed them. She joked to her doctor that "if I had one thought that there was an iota of truth in the [Summersby] affair, I would have gone after [the handsome General Montgomery]. And believe you me, my friend, I could have gotten him!"

✦

Decades after her tenure as First Lady, Mrs. Eisenhower told Rosalynn Carter in 1977, "I loved being in the White House. . . . [But then] I was never expected to do all the things you have to do."

JACQUELINE KENNEDY

b. 1929   d. 1994

First Lady
JANUARY 20, 1961–NOVEMBER 22, 1963

t a young age, Jacqueline "Jackie" Lee
Bouvier Kennedy enjoyed creative writing,
illustrating, and studying ballet in addition
to riding horses. During the winter of 1947 she
was titled "the Debutante of the Year." However,
she continued her studies, first at Vassar, then
at the Sorbonne, where she developed her love of

the French and an internationally oriented attitude, and later graduated from George Washington University. She met the capital's most eligible bachelor—Senator John F. Kennedy—while working as a newspaper photographer. They married in 1953.

Mrs. Kennedy was a tireless champion of the arts during her time as First Lady. She assisted in developing plans for a national cultural center, known today as the John F. Kennedy Center for the Performing Arts. She also redecorated the White House with the philosophy of creating a living historical monument to America in addition to a pleasant home for the First Family. Her impact was so extensive that some historians and decorators refer to the White House as B.J. and A.J.— Before Jackie and After Jackie.

When President Kennedy was shot in Dallas, Texas, on November 22, 1963, Mrs. Kennedy's unfaltering dignity and courage earned her international respect and admiration. Her life and the lives of her children, Caroline and John Jr., received no respite from the press thereafter. The flattery of being the nation's darling and fashion trendsetter no longer interested Mrs. Kennedy, who longed for privacy. The former First Lady married Aristotle Onassis, a wealthy and powerful businessman, in 1968. After his death she worked at the publishing house Doubleday, where she specialized in books on Egyptian art as well as literature and the performing arts. At her funeral in

1994, John Jr. eulogized her three defining characteristics: her "love of words, the bonds of home and family, and her spirit of adventure."

Mrs. Kennedy once remarked that her job description was primarily "to take care of the President."

"If you bungle raising your children, I don't think whatever else you do well matters very much."

When Jackie was very young, she went for a stroll in Central Park with her nine-month-old sister Lee and their nurse. Somehow, Jackie wandered off, and a policeman noticed her alone. She walked right up to him and announced, "My nurse and baby sister seem to be lost."

"I was a tomboy," she recalled, in 1962. "I decided to learn to dance and I became feminine."

As a high school student at the exclusive Miss Porter's, she wrote to a friend, "I just know no one will ever marry me and I'll end up as a house mother in Farmington."

After her junior year at the Sorbonne in France, she toured Italy. She wrote her stepfather: "All the places and feelings and happiness that bind you to a family you love are something you take with you no matter how far you go."

Around the same time, she told her step-brother, "I have to write Mummy a ream each week or she gets hysterical and thinks I'm dead or married to an Italian."

⌒

Before she met Mr. Kennedy, she attended all sorts of parties and dances. She remembered, "They were okay. But Newport—when I was about nineteen, I knew I didn't want the rest of my life to be there. I didn't want to marry any of the young men I grew up with—not because of them, but because of their life. I didn't know what I wanted. I was still floundering."

⌒

In 1952, at the age of twenty-two, Mrs. Kennedy took a job as "Inquiring Photographer" at *The Washington Times-Herald.* The questions she formulated were quite unusual:

"Chaucer said that what women most desire is power over men. What do you think women desire most?"

"If you were going to be executed tomorrow morning, what would you order for your last meal on earth?"

"Would you like to crash high society?"

"Do the rich enjoy life more than the poor?"

"Do you think a wife should let her husband think he's smarter than she is?"

"How do you feel when you get a wolf whistle?"

Today, some of her other questions seem to verge on the prophetic:

"Which First Lady would you most like to have been?"

"Would you like your son to grow up to be President?"

"If you had a date with Marilyn Monroe, what would you talk about?"

"Should a candidate's wife campaign with her husband?"

"What prominent person's death affected you most?"

The day came for her to interview the man she was dating, Senator Kennedy, for her column. She actually asked him, "Can you give any reason why a contented bachelor would want to get married?"

⟳

During her whirlwind courtship with the dashing Mr. Kennedy, she told a friend, "I'm the luckiest girl in the world. Mummy is terrified of Jack because she can't push him around at all." But her father, the rough-and-tumble stockbroker "Black Jack" Bouvier, got along pretty well with Mr. Kennedy. "They talk," Mrs. Kennedy recalled, "about sports, politics, and women—what all red-blooded men like to talk about." Years later, she complained to a friend that her sister Lee "is so dippy about Jack it's sickening."

✕

During the early months of their courtship, she recalls, "He'd call me from some oyster bar up on the Cape with a great clinking of coins, to ask me out to the movies the following Wednesday."

✕

The couple's early relationship endured break-ups, delays, and all sorts of misunderstandings, along with some wonderful times. She once joked, "I don't know if I'll live long enough to marry him."

✕

She once told dinner companions that to her, the most important thing about a man "is that he must weigh more and have bigger feet than I do."

✕

When she and Mr. Kennedy finally became engaged, here's how she told one relative about it: "Aunt Maudie, I just want you to know that I'm engaged to Jack Kennedy. But you can't tell any-one for a while because it wouldn't be fair to *The Saturday Evening Post*."

"What does *The Saturday Evening Post* have to do with it?" her aunt asked.

"The *Post* is coming out tomorrow with an article on Jack. And the title is right on the cover. It's 'Jack Kennedy—the Senate's Gay Young Bachelor.'"

ॐ

One reporter asked her at the time of her engagement if she felt she had much in common with her fiancé. She told the reporter, "Since Jack is such a violently independent person, and I, too, am so independent, this relationship will take a lot of working out."

ॐ

She first met the sprawling Kennedy clan in Hyannis Port. "How can I explain these people?" she later asked a friend. "They were like carbonated water, and other families might be flat. They'd be talking about so many things with so much enthusiasm. Or they'd be playing games. At dinner or in the living room, anywhere, everybody would be talking about something. They had so much interest in life—it was so stimulating. And so gay and so open and accepting. They even compete with each other in conversation to see who can say the most and talk the loudest."

On another occasion, she said, "The day you become engaged to one of them is the day they start saying how 'fantastic' you are, and the same loyalty they show to each other they show to their in-laws. They are so proud when one of them does well."

ॐ

"The first time I met [Rose Kennedy] was about a year, a little more than a year, before I married Jack, when I came that summer for a weekend. I remember she was terribly sweet to me. For instance, I had a sort of special dress to wear to dinner—I was more dressed up than his sisters were, and so Jack teased me about it, in an affectionate way, but he said something like, 'Where do you think you're going?' She said, 'Oh, don't be mean to her, dear. She looks lovely.'"

⤲

In 1960, she reflected on newly appointed Attorney General Robert Kennedy: "Bobby is immensely ambitious and will never feel that he has succeeded in life until he has been elected to something, even mayor of Hyannis Port. Being appointed to office isn't enough."

Bobby was to be a great help to Mrs. Kennedy and her children over the course of his tragically short life. She once noted, "I think he is the most compassionate person I know, but probably only the closest people around him—family, friends, and those who work for him—would see that. People of a private nature are often misunderstood because they are too shy and too proud to explain themselves."

⤲

She had somewhat less kind things to say about Ethel Kennedy. Truman Capote once quoted her as referring to Ethel as "the baby-making machine—wind her up and she becomes pregnant." On another occasion, she said Ethel "drops kids like rabbits." And she told her sister Lee Radziwell that Ethel was "the type who would put a slip cover on a Louis Quinze sofa and then spell it Louie Cans."

჻

As for Teddy, here's how Mrs. Kennedy sized him up in 1959: "Ted is such a little boy in so many ways. The way he almost puffs himself up when he talks to Jack. He hero-worships him, of course. I think it was only last year that Ted started calling him Jack, and I think he first asked if he could. But there's been such a change in him. He used to be so terribly, terribly serious all the time, but now he relaxes a little more, smiles a little more, and he's still very serious. But he's so very nice and so very intelligent."

჻

Mrs. Kennedy was more attuned to Joan Kennedy than the other women in the Kennedy clan. "In the beginning," she said, "Joan was so happy with Ted. Whenever we were all in Hyannis Port, you could see the pride on Ted's face when she walked in the room with her great figure and her leopard-skin outfits. If only she had realized her own strengths instead of looking at herself in comparison with the Kennedys. Why worry if you're not as good at tennis as Eunice or Ethel when men are attracted by the feminine way you play tennis? Why court Ethel's tennis elbow?"

❧

But the famous Kennedy dynasty troubled Mrs. Kennedy as well. "Wait till I introduce Jack Kennedy to Aunt Edie [her aunt Edith Bouvier Beale, a deeply eccentric woman who lived in East Hampton in utter squalor with dozens of cats]. You know, I doubt if he'd survive it. The Kennedys are terribly bourgeois."

❧

On another occasion, she remarked that "Just watching [the Kennedys] wore me out." She told her sister that the famous roughness of the competitive games the Kennedys played dismayed her considerably. "They'll kill me before I ever get to marry him. I swear they will."

❧

Before the wedding day finally came in 1953, she famously said, "What I want more than anything else in the world is to be married to him."

❧

She recalled, "During our first year of marriage we were like gypsies living in and out of a suitcase. It was turbulent. Jack made speeches all over the country and was never home more than two nights a week. To make matters even more restless, we had rented a house in Georgetown for six months, and when the lease ran out, we moved to a hotel. We spent the summer, off and on, at Jack's father's house in Hyannis Port. Ours was the little room on the first floor that Jack used to have by himself. It didn't take me long to realize it was only big enough for one."

The many difficulties of being married to a politician all seemed to surface during their first year of marriage. "I was alone almost every weekend," she recalled. "It was all wrong. Politics was sort of my enemy, and we had no home life whatsoever."

When an interviewer asked Mrs. Kennedy in 1954 what were her theories for a good marriage, she replied a bit dourly, "I can't say I have any yet."

ॐ

Still, after they'd been married a while, Mrs. Kennedy felt they'd made a successful match. In 1957, she said, "I brought a certain amount of order to his life. We had good food in our house— not merely the bare staples that he used to have. He no longer went out in the morning with one brown shoe and one black shoe on. His clothes got pressed and he got to the airport without a mad rush because I packed for him. I can be helpful packing suitcases, laying out clothes, rescuing lost coats and luggage. It's those little things that make you tired."

ॐ

She also said, "The thing that gives me the greatest satisfaction is making the house run absolutely smoothly so that Jack can come home early or late and bring as many unexpected guests as he likes. Frankly, this takes quite a bit of planning."

જી

She said frequently, "I separate politics from my private life. Maybe that's why I treasure my life at home so much."

જી

After they'd been married for about three years, in 1956, Mrs. Kennedy told a reporter, "I wouldn't say that being married to a very busy politician is the easiest life to adjust to. But you think about it and figure out the best way to do things—to keep the house running smoothly, to spend as much time as you can with your husband and your children—and eventually you find yourself well adjusted. The most important thing for a successful marriage is for a husband to do what he likes best and does well. The wife's satisfaction will follow."

જી

By 1958, Mrs. Kennedy was singing a somewhat different tune about politics. "Politics is in my blood," she said. "I know that even if Jack changed professions, I would miss politics. It's the most exciting life imaginable—always involved with the news of the moment, meeting and working with people who are enormously alive, and every day you are caught up in something you really care about. It makes a lot of other things seem less vital. You get used to the pressure that never lets up, and you learn to live with it as a fish lives in water."

❧

"I think every woman wants to be needed, and in politics, you are."

❧

During the beginnings of the presidential campaign in 1959, she said, "I married a whirlwind. He's indestructible. People who try to keep up with him drop like flies, including me. It sounds endless and it is. The first two days [of the campaign] were the hardest—but then I got into the rhythm of it." And this: "If Jack didn't run for President, he'd be like a tiger in a cage."

❧

At around the same time, she said, "It's not easy, this traveling, but we are together and he tells me how much it helps him just for me to be there. And I try to be natural with people. I think if you aren't, then they sense it immediately."

❧

After JFK got the nomination of his party for President, Mrs. Kennedy, pregnant with John Jr., told reporters about how she saw her role from then on in: "I suppose I won't be able to play much part in the campaign, but I'll do what I can. I feel I should be with Jack when he's engaged in

such a struggle, and if it weren't for the baby, I'd
campaign even more vigorously than Mrs. Nixon.
I can't be so presumptuous as to think I could
have any effect on the outcome, but it would be so
tragic if my husband lost by a few votes merely
because I wasn't at his side and because people
had met Mrs. Nixon and liked her."

༄

After her husband won the presidency, Mrs.
Kennedy described her notions of the role of the
political wife: "You have to do what your husband wants you to do. My life revolves around
my husband. His life is my life. It is up to me to
make his home a haven, a refuge, to arrange it
so that he can see as much of me and his children as possible—but never let the arrangements ruffle him, never let him see that it is
work. I want to take such good care of my
husband that, whatever he is doing, he can
do better because he has me. His work is so
important."

༄

Mrs. Kennedy frequently provided literary
allusions and quotations for her husband's
speeches. "I thought of some lines from a poem I
thought he ought to use, and he told me to get the
rest of it. I used to worry myself sick when Jack
said to me that he didn't know what he was going
to say in his next speech, but now, even though he
still says it sometimes, it doesn't bother me

because he has picked up so much more self-confidence in himself and his speechmaking that he can get up without any speech and I absolutely know he'll be all right without fumbling for thoughts or anything because he has so much in his head and he has real presence. I think it's a compliment that I listen to his speeches the way I do because he always has some fresh things to say at the beginning of each speech, things that nobody knows he was going to say. Even in the things he'd said before, the sections of speeches, he always changes them somehow so that each time it's just a bit different."

꒒

"You shake hundreds of hands in the afternoon and hundreds more at night. You get so tired you catch yourself laughing and crying at the same time. But you pace yourself and you get through it. You just look at it as something you have to do. You knew it would come and you knew it was worth it. The places blur after a while, they really do. I remember people, not faces, in a receiving line. The thing you get from these people is a sense of shyness and anxiety and shining expectancy. These women who come up to see me at a meeting, they're as shy as I am. Sometimes we just stand there smiling at each other and just don't say anything."

꒒

When Mr. Kennedy won the presidency, Mrs.

Kennedy started panicking about her impending official duties. She told a good friend, "I'll get pregnant and stay pregnant. It's the only way out."

∽

Mrs. Kennedy joined the majority of First Ladies in despising the White House, perhaps the most vehemently of all. Certainly she had a tremendous impact on the building, and talked about it more than anyone previously had on the record.

After Mamie Eisenhower gave her the first grand tour, she exclaimed, "Oh, God. It's the worst place in the world. So cold and dreary. A dungeon like the Lubyanka. It looks like it's been furnished by discount stores. I've never seen anything like it. I can't bear the thought of moving in. I hate it, hate it, hate it."

∽

"The minute I knew that Jack was going to run for President, I knew the White House would be one of my main projects if he won."

∽

She complained extensively to Hugh Sidey in a *Life* magazine feature: "[The White House is] like a hotel. Everywhere I look there is somebody standing around or walking down a hall."

"Like any President's wife," she continued, "I'm here for only a brief time. And before everything slips away, before every link with the past is gone, I want to do this. I want to find all the

people who are still here who know about the
White House, were intimate with it—the nephews,
the sons, the great-grandchildren, the people who
are still living and remember things about the
White House. It has been fascinating to go
through the building with Mrs. Nicholas
Longworth, who was Theodore Roosevelt's daughter, and with Franklin D. Roosevelt Jr., and
President Truman, and hear them tell where
things had been placed in their day."

ༀ

Privately, however, she said, "It looks like a
house where nothing has taken place. There is no
trace of the past."

ༀ

Publicly, Mrs. Kennedy gave a more detailed
explanation: "I think the White House should
show the wonderful heritage that this country has.
We had such a wonderful flowering in the late
eighteenth century. And the restoration is so fascinating—every day you see a letter that has come
in from the great-great grandson of a President. It
was such a surprise to come here and find so little
that had association and memory. I'd feel terribly
if I lived here for four years and hadn't done anything for the house."

ༀ

"I felt like a moth banging on the windowpane
when I first moved into [the White House]. It was
terrible. You couldn't even open the windows in

the rooms because they hadn't been opened for years. The shades you pulled down at night were so enormous that they had pulleys and ropes. When we tried the fireplaces, they smoked because they hadn't ever been used. Sometimes I wondered, 'How are we going to live as a family in this enormous place?' I'm afraid it will always be a little impossible for the people who live there. It's an office building."

⤳

"I just think that everything in the White House should be the best, the entertainment that's given here, and if it's an American company that you can help, I like to do that. If it's not, just as long as it's the best."

⤳

"When I first moved into the White House, I thought, I wish I could be married to Thomas Jefferson, because he would know best what should be done to it. But then I thought, no, Presidents' wives have an obligation to contribute something, so this will be the thing I will work hardest at myself.

"How could I help wanting to do it? I don't know. Is it a reverence for beauty or for history? I guess both. I've always cared. My best friends are people who care. I don't know. . . . When you read Proust or listen to Jack talk about history or go to Mount Vernon, you understand. I feel strongly about the children who come here. When I think about my own son and how to make him turn out like his father, I think of Jack's great sense of history."

✧

Her memos to White House staff, including this one to the chief usher, J. B. West, certainly give a strong sense of that impact:

"If there's anything I can't stand, it's Victorian mirrors—they're hideous—off to the dungeons with them. Have them removed and relegated to the junk heap.

"No Mamie pink on the walls except in Caroline's room, no Grand Rapids reconditioned furniture, no glass-and-brass ashtrays or trinkets—I intend to make this a grand house.

"I can't teach the maids anything—nor have time to—when they are that scared, they are too panicky to remember. The only way they will get to be good maids is to be around the family and house enough so that some of the terror leaves them."

✧

Elsewhere in the Hugh Sidey *Life* magazine feature, she talked about her vision of the restoration of the White House. "All these people come to see the White House, and they see practically nothing that dates back before 1948. Every boy who comes here should see things that develop his sense of history. For the girls, the house should look beautiful and lived-in. They should see what a fire in the fireplace and pretty flowers can do for a house; the White House rooms should give them a sense of all that. Everything in the White House must have a reason for being there. It would be sacrilege merely to 'redecorate' it—a word I hate. It must be restored—and that has nothing to do with decoration. That is a question of scholarship."

✺

To the decorator she selected (Sister Parrish) to redo the private living quarters in the White House, Mrs. Kennedy said: "Let's have lots of chintz and gay up this old dump." And: "I never want a house where you have to say to the children, 'Don't touch.'"

✺

She showed a certain fondness for the second-story Oval Room. In 1961, she said, "This is a beautiful room. I love it most. There is this magnificent view. It means something to the man who stands there and sees it—after all he's done to get there."

✺

"People have told me ninety-nine things that I had to do as First Lady, and I haven't done one of them."

✺

"What I wanted to do more than anything was to keep my family together. I didn't want to go down into coal mines or be a symbol of elegance. I just wanted to save some normal life for Jack and the children and for me. My first fight was to fight for a sane life for my babies and their father."

⌒

Mrs. Kennedy felt besieged by sightseers— because she was. She asked that more shrubbery be planted by the White House fence to obscure the view from the street. "I'm sick and tired of starring in everybody's home movies," she said.

⌒

On another occasion, she told a friend, "I can't bear all those people peering over the fence. Eunice loves the whole horrible business. I may abdicate."

⌒

Indeed, the visual accessibility of the White House became quite a fixation for Mrs. Kennedy. She did extensive personal research to find the precise point in the high wrought-iron fence around the White House where tourists and press photographers could take photos of the children at play. She wrote a memo to the White House usher, J. B. West, and included a vivid diagram of the White House lawn. She wrote, "If you stand in the children's playground—you will see that lots of people can take photographs from the place marked X." After requesting that a "solid wall" of trees or shrubs be installed there, she continued,

"Who will be the first President brave enough to build a brick wall?"

⟳

In fact, as most everyone knows, the central obsession in Mrs. Kennedy's life was privacy. It was a lifelong obsession, but living in the fishbowl that the White House was in the 1960s and is, to some extent, to this day, exacerbated her worst fears. But those fears began before she was installed in the White House.

When Mr. Kennedy was nominated by his party, she moaned, "I'm still only thirty years old, and I've just lost my anonymity for good. It's a little scary."

After the election, she wrote to her friend, designer Oleg Cassini: "PROTECT ME—as I seem so mercilessly exposed and don't know how to cope with it. (I read tonight I dye my hair because it is mousy gray!)"

Shortly after moving into the White House, Mrs. Kennedy wrote a memo to her press secretary Pam Turnure on the policy of secrecy, in which she wrote, "I feel strongly that publicity in this era has gotten completely out of hand—and you must really protect the privacy of me and my children—but not offend [the media]. My press relations will be minimum information given with maximum politeness. . . . I won't give any interviews—pose for any photographs, etc.—for the next four years."

✌

She later reflected, "Sometimes I think you become sort of a—there ought to be a nicer word than *freak,* but I can't think of one."

✌

Mrs. Kennedy had this amusing exchange with reporters in 1960:

"When you are First Lady," one reporter told her, "you won't be able to jump into your car and rush down to Orange County to go fox hunting."

"You couldn't be more wrong," Mrs. Kennedy replied. "That is one thing I won't ever give up."

"But you'll have to make some concessions to the role, won't you?"

"Oh, I will. I'll wear hats."

✌

When she could become philosophical about being such a public figure, she had a certain ironic eloquence. "When you get written about a lot," she once said, "you just think of it as a little cartoon that runs along at the bottom of your life—but one that doesn't have much to do with your life."

✌

"Why should I traipse around playing Lady Bountiful when I have so much to do here to make this house livable?"

✌

"I never allowed myself to think he would lose the election. My husband said he would win, and I'm an old-fashioned kind of wife who believes her husband."

～

"It never hurts a child to read something that may be above his head. Books written down for children often do not awaken a dormant curiosity."

～

"I believe that if you can't cope with emergencies by the time you are twenty-five, you'll never be able to adapt yourself to situations."

～

She reflected late in life, "It was most difficult, our first year of marriage. Being married to a Senator, you have to adjust to the fact that the only routine is no routine."

～

"Being a fashion leader is at the very bottom of the list of things I desire."

～

When her husband (and certain members of the press) complained about her rather extravagant spending, she responded by saying, "I have to dress well, Jack, so I won't embarrass you. As a public figure you'd be humiliated if I were photographed in some saggy old housedress. Everyone would say your wife is a slob and refuse to vote for you."

⌒

A Manhattan trade paper held that Mrs. Kennedy was "too chic." The paper claimed that she and her mother-in-law Rose spent $30,000 a year buying Paris frocks. Mrs. Kennedy was enraged. "I couldn't spend that much unless I wore sable underwear," she snapped.

⌒

She cleverly used the fabled televised White House tour to defend herself on this issue. Host Charles Collingwood asked if all the pieces in the Lincoln Bedroom were from Lincoln's time. "Yes, they are," she replied. "The most famous one, of course, is the Lincoln bed. Every President seemed to love it. Theodore Roosevelt slept in it. So did Calvin Coolidge. It's probably the most famous piece of furniture in the White House. It was bought by Mrs. Lincoln along with the dressing bureaus and chair and this table. She bought a lot of furniture for this house. She made her husband rather cross because he thought she spent too much money."

⌒

On another occasion, she defended herself this way: "I don't understand it. Jack will spend any amount of money to buy votes, but he balks at investing a thousand dollars in a beautiful painting."

❧

"It takes an awful lot of effort to make everything look effortless."

❧

"I don't really like to call attention to anything. I think I'm more of a private person."

❧

"It's terribly creative to make a house a happy place to live in."

❧

"I care terribly about making a home a sanctuary."

❧

"The White House is an eighteenth- and nineteenth-century house and should be kept as a period house. Whatever one does, one does gradually, to make a house a more lived-in house with beautiful things of its period. I would write fifty letters to fifty museum curators if I could bring Andrew Jackson's inkwell home."

❧

"Housekeeping is a joy to me. I feel that this is what I was made for. When it all runs smoothly, when the food is good and the flowers look fresh, I have such satisfaction."

❧

"I want to take such good care of my husband that whatever he is doing, he can do it better because he has me."

⟡

"All this talk over what I wear and how I fix my hair has amused and puzzled me. What does my hairdo have to do with my husband's ability to be President?"

⟡

"Happiness is not where you think you find it. I'm determined not to worry. So many people poison every day worrying about the next. I've learned a lot from my husband."

⟡

"I certainly would not express any views that were not my husband's. I get all my views from him. Not because I can't make up my own mind on my own, but because he would not be where he is unless he was one of the most able men in his party, so I think he's right."

⟡

One of Mrs. Kennedy's most famous remarks: "American history is for men."

⟡

"A sense of history and ability to learn from the past is of prime importance in any man in a position of leadership today."

❧

"I have to contribute in every way I can to the elevation of the arts in our country."

❧

"My major effort must be devoted to my children. I feel very strongly that if they do not grow up as happy and secure individuals—if Caroline and John turn out badly—nothing that I would accomplish in the public eye would give me any satisfaction."

❧

"I am not sure I share the supposed dream of American women to see their sons be President. Being President is one thing. You could not help but be proud of that. But running for office is another—an ordeal you would wish to spare sons and husbands. You worry and wish you could diminish the strain, but, of course, you cannot."

❧

"I don't think there are any men who are faithful to their wives."

❧

"Being in the White House does make friendship difficult. I do try to have a few friends for dinner as often as possible. Mostly it turns out to be someone we know really well, because I hate to call and have people feel they have to come."

❧

Mrs. Kennedy tired of her husband's continual groaning and complaining about his overwhelming responsibilities and problems whenever the two of them were alone for dinner. She seemed unable to regard national problems as her problems. One night, a White House butler allegedly overheard the couple just as dinner was served. "What in hell am I ever going to do about air pollution?"

Furious, Mrs. Kennedy replied, "It's very simple, my dear. Get the Air Force to spray our industrial centers with Chanel Number Five."

ᴣ

"As women, we should exert our great influence in the cause of world peace."

ᴣ

In 1963, after her husband was assassinated and before she pulled herself together enough to leave the White House, she provided mementos to friends and members of the staff. She told Godfrey McHugh: "First I didn't want in, now I can't seem to leave."

ᴣ

Two years after the assassination of her husband, Mrs. Kennedy wrote: "Learning to accept what was unthinkable changes you."

ᴣ

In 1968, when Mrs. Kennedy was forty, she shocked most of the world when she announced her engagement to sixty-year-old Aristotle Onassis.

A friend warned her, "Jackie, you're going to fall off your pedestal."

"That's better than freezing there," she replied.

৵

In his touching eulogy delivered at his sister-in-law's funeral mass, Teddy Kennedy remembered something she'd said to him when the Clintons visited Martha's Vineyard in the summer of 1993. "When we were waiting for President and Mrs. Clinton to arrive, Jackie turned to me and said, 'Teddy, you go down and greet the President.' But I said, 'Maurice is already there.' And Jackie said, 'Teddy, you do it. Maurice isn't running for reelection.'"

LADY BIRD JOHNSON

b. 1912

First Lady

NOVEMBER 22, 1963–JANUARY 20, 1969

C laudia Alta "Lady Bird" Taylor Johnson's father raised her to have good business sense. After graduating from the University of Texas, she met Lyndon Baines Johnson while he was a congressional secretary visiting Texas. Seven weeks after that first meeting in 1934, after intense correspondence between

Austin, Texas, and Washington, D.C., he proposed.
They were married within the year. As Mrs.
Johnson later put it, "Sometimes Lyndon simply
takes your breath away." She often helped out in
his office while his political career blossomed. Her
steady managerial hand became particularly influential when she assisted his staff during his recu-
peration from a severe heart attack while he was
Majority Leader of the Senate. He said of his
beloved wife that voters "would happily have
elected her over me."

As the wife of the Vice-President, Mrs. Johnson
visited thirty-three foreign countries. Faced with
the national tragedy of President Kennedy's assassination, she led the country through the grieving
process and the time of political transition. Mrs.
Johnson championed her husband's war-on-
poverty campaign and the Head Start project. She
may have first been nicknamed "Lady Bird" when
quite young, but her support of nature conservation as an adult earned her the title. She started a
First Lady's Committee for a More Beautiful
Capital and later broadened the initiative to
include the whole country. She founded the
National Wildflower Research Center in 1982 and
continues to support that organization as well as
the Lyndon Baines Johnson Library and the
National Geographic Society.

"My image will emerge in deeds, not in words."

✌

"If I had known this was going to happen to me, I would have changed my nose and my nickname."

✌

"What you can do may never see the light of print. It is the integrity that comes from attempting without fuss or self-preoccupation to see a good job well done. Its value is the work itself, what you have given others, whether your product is a better school in Harlem, or an inspired husband and children, or both."

✌

"Everything we do begins at home. Each of us is action-sprung from what nurtures us."

✌

"In this space age, passive citizenship is a luxury no one can afford. Our challenge is to seize the burdens of our generation and make them lighter for those who follow us."

✌

Mrs. Johnson was asked at a news conference what it was she "really" did: "Actually, the question is one that every woman, and especially every wife involved in public duties, frequently asks herself . . . you just hope that all your efforts add up to something worthwhile."

✌

When asked about her aims when her husband was Vice President, she replied, "Helping Lyndon all that I can, helping Mrs. Kennedy whenever she needs me, and becoming a more alive me."

⌇

"I can't say that a solid diet of success is good for anyone."

⌇

"Every politician should have been born an orphan and remain a bachelor."

⌇

Well known as a financial whiz, Mrs. Johnson once said, "I wouldn't have a joint checking account with the Angel Gabriel."

⌇

"Success has many faces; it need not be circumscribed by a title, a job, a cause. Success is not always 'getting.' It is more often 'giving.' It does not consist of what we do, but rather in what we are. Success is not always an accomplishment. It can be a state of mind. The quiet dignity of a home, the relationship of the individuals in the home. The continuing expression of an inquiring mind can mean more in terms of success than all the surface symbols of status."

⌇

"Sometimes silence is the greatest sin."

❧

"You can't run the country if you can't run yourself."

❧

"A thing means so much more if it's shared."

❧

"The well-written word is man's most useful instrument—the way the superior mind catches human experience and reshapes the insignificant particulars into a pattern that has meaning for us all."

❧

"I believe that one of the great problems for us as individuals is the depression and the tension resulting from existence in a world which is increasingly less pleasing to the eye."

❧

"We—as a nation—have just begun to accept beauty as a necessity to our vocabulary."

❧

"The sound of laughter marks the soaring spirit."

❧

"Every once in a while I yearn for nothing to do. But then, of course, I realize I'm glad I'm busy. There's so *much* for Americans to do today."

❧

Mrs. Johnson's hairdos were controversial, to put it nicely. But she maintained, "I like to think that what's in a person's head is more important than what is outside."

࿐

"I like clothes I can depend on. They should be few in number, easy to care for, and take well to lots of travel. I don't like clothes that must be babied."

࿐

"If you can achieve the precious balance between women's domestic and civil life, you can do more for zest and sanity in our society than by any other achievement."

࿐

"I think people can assess a man a little in relation to what kind of wife and family he has."

࿐

"The only thing I can say is that marriage, like life, is never static."

࿐

"Today a woman with the strength to take on problems that do not lend themselves to quick and easy solutions can build the success that comes of fulfillment, of a cause won, and a world the better for it."

࿐

"Woman can no longer afford to concern herself only with the hearth—any more than man can afford to concern himself only with his job."

✧

When asked whether she felt American women dominate men, Mrs. Johnson said, "American women have been partners since pioneer days. There's no question of domination on either side."

✧

"I believe that the educated woman today has a role to play—of courage and conviction—unparalleled since frontier times."

✧

"To me, the greatest contribution of women from Eve to 1961 is twofold: continuity and idealism."

✧

"A quite remarkable young woman has been emerging in the United States. She might be the complete woman. She has taken over the right to participate fully in the life of the community. She wants to be—while being equally involved—preeminently a woman, a wife, a mother, a thinking citizen."

✧

"American women are undergoing a quiet revolution in our lifetime. We have learned to master dishwashers, typewriters, and voting machines with reasonable aplomb. We must now try to make our laws catch up with what has happened to us as we bounce in and out of the labor market and raise a family."

＊

"I think we have reached the point in our national lives when the affluence and leisure time and the technology have all come together, when we can apply ourselves and look around us and try to keep for our children and our grandchildren what we have loved and enjoyed."

＊

"Never before have young women found it so full of opportunity to achieve, so full of challenge to be creative. In every community there is a need for women leaders, women with a gift of understanding, women with vision, women with confidence in themselves, women with a questing mind and a quiet heart."

＊

"One fear—the closest to the female heart of twenty—is the fear that your intelligence is a threat to your femininity—that whatever you may achieve in your chosen work outside the home competes dangerously with your desirability as wife and mother. It can, but it needn't."

＊

"Natural beauty may be a national concern and there is much that government can and should do, but it is the individual who not only benefits, but must protect a heritage of beauty for future generations."

✌

"We have come to learn it is far easier to cut down a tree than to grow one. It is far easier to pollute a river than to restore it. It is far easier to devastate a flowering countryside than to make it bloom again."

✌

"[Teenagers in the mid-1960s] are more aware of and concerned about their place in the world and the dawning tomorrow. I think they are living in the most important period of mankind's life on this planet, with more potential for good on the one hand and a lowering cloud of Armageddon on the other."

✌

"We all want to eliminate the ugly fences of poverty which cut off so many pastures of opportunity. We all want to provide adequate education for the young and adequate medical care for the aging and to protect the natural beauty which a generous Providence has bestowed on us."

✌

"In the war on poverty, as we have raised the curtain on some of our most blighted conditions, we have come to know how essential beauty is to the human spirit. You can find the human craving for it in small things and large."

✂

In June 1964, LBJ and Mrs. Johnson hosted a state dinner for the Danish Prime Minister and his wife. It was their daughter Luci's first state dinner, and they all enjoyed themselves enormously. But the evening didn't quite end when the music and dancing stopped, as Mrs. Johnson confided in her diary:

> And then late at night, after everybody was gone, occurred one of my funniest little moments in the White House. In my robe and slippers, ready for bed, I observed that all the lights in the second-floor hall were still on, and I went from one to the other, turning them off. When I got to the staircase that leads down to the State floor, I could hear a few clattering feet below disappearing in the distance, and I could see a great blaze of light going down the steps. If I could step out into the hall only a few feet I could turn off the main lights, but I was afraid the door would lock behind me.
>
> Cautiously I pushed the door open, held it with my foot, reached as far as I could—it was quite obvious I couldn't get to the switch. Some giddy instinct of daring led me to just let the door close gently and to walk over and turn out the lights. Then I went back and turned the knob—and sure enough the door

was locked tight! I knocked, hoping maybe
the guests in the Queen's Room would hear
me. I called gently, I called a little louder,
nobody heard me! There was no sound below
now, but there were a few lights still on. I
thought about all those funny ads—"I went to
the Opera in my Maidenform Bra"—and I
thought how awful it would be if I walked
through the main entrance hall of the White
House at about 1:30, in my dressing gown,
and met a dozen or so of the departing
guests. But there was nothing else to do, so
with a very assured look (I hope!) I went
walking down the stairs and through the hall
where I met only two or three of the departing musicians and staff members. I smiled as
if the whole thing were a matter of course,
caught the elevator back up to my own floor,
and so to bed, thinking this had been a
remarkable day in many ways.

⬏

"In a country founded, in part, by a man who
was daring enough to say that we were devoted to
life, liberty, and the pursuit of happiness—he
ranked the pursuit of happiness right up there at
the top. And beauty and happiness are certainly
inextricably tied together."

⬏

"Politics was Lyndon's life, not mine, and
thirty-seven years were enough."

❧

"Art is the window to man's soul. Without it, he would never be able to see beyond his immediate world; nor could the world see the man within."

❧

"I'll know I am growing old when I no longer thrill to the first snow of the season."

PAT NIXON

b. 1912   d. 1993

First Lady
JANUARY 20, 1969–AUGUST 8, 1974

Thelma Catherine Patricia "Pat" Ryan Nixon took on the responsibilities as the matriarch of her working-class family after her mother died when Pat was only thirteen. When she was eighteen, her father died. Determined to get her degree, she worked her way through junior college and eventually graduated cum laude from the University of Southern California in 1937. She then taught high school. "She was a quiet inspiration perhaps, to our secret hopes," a former student once commented—"there was something about her which made us want to be as much like her as possible." While teaching, she met and married Richard Nixon, whom she supported through good times and bad, including the Watergate scandal of his presidency. She steadfastly said, "I love my husband. I believe in him, and I am proud of his accomplishments."

Mrs. Nixon campaigned with her husband so productively that they were known as the "Pat and Dick Team." While Mr. Nixon was in public office, his wife visited more than eighty countries, often traveling alone on humanitarian missions. She scheduled a minimum of formal receptions on those trips to have more time for visiting orphanages, hospitals, victims of natural disasters, and once even a Panamanian leper colony. Mrs. Nixon became the first First Lady to visit a combat zone (in an open helicopter, no less) when she accompanied her husband to South Vietnam. She also encouraged volunteer service and supported the "Right to Read" program.

Pat Nixon collected more than 600 paintings and antiques for the White House and placed emphasis on making her home accessible to the American public. Historian William Seale said, "The great collection of White House Americana today is the long shadow of Mrs. Nixon. The impulse, the idea, and the energy were hers." She arranged candlelit tours for people who worked during the day and facilitated tours for the hearing and visually impaired. She also initiated the practice of lighting the White House from the outside like other national monuments. She died in 1993.

When she was asked about her dreams and goals as a girl, Mrs. Nixon replied with surprising passion, "I never had time to think about things like that—who I wanted to be or who I admired, or to have ideas. I had to work . . . I've never had it easy."

"[Richard] wakes up during the night, switches on the light, speaks into his tape recorder or takes notes—it's impossible. No one could sleep in the same bed with Dick."

"I do or die. I never cancel out."

Mr. Nixon once said, "I remember through all of our campaigns, whether it was a receiving line or whether it was going to a face in the airport, she was the one that always insisted on shaking that last hand, not simply because she was thinking of that vote, but because she simply could not turn down that last child or that last person."

❧

"In this job, you know a lot. But you have to keep quiet."

❧

Mrs. Nixon told Gloria Steinem during a probing interview in 1968, "I don't have time to worry about who I admire or who I identify with. I'm not like all you—all those people who had it easy."

BETTY FORD

b. 1918

First Lady
AUGUST 8, 1974–JANUARY 20, 1977

Elizabeth "Betty" Bloomer Warren Ford majored in dance in college and eventually made a career of it, studying with Martha Graham and performing in her group as well as working as a fashion model in New York City. After moving back to her hometown of Grand

Rapids, Michigan, she taught dance to handicapped children and worked as a fashion coordinator for a department store. She married Gerald
Ford two weeks before he was elected to Congress
in 1948. Twenty-five years of political life later,
Betty Ford looked forward to retirement, but then
her husband was surprisingly selected as Vice
President and soon thereafter took over as com-
mander in chief when Nixon resigned.

As First Lady, Mrs. Ford was honest and open
about her fight with breast cancer, which did
much to increase awareness. She underwent radi-
cal surgery in 1974 and explained that "maybe if I
as First Lady could talk about it candidly and
without embarrassment, many other people would
be able to as well." She cochaired the Susan G.
Komen Foundation at its inception and continues
to support the organization. Mrs. Ford also advo-
cated the Equal Rights Amendment while in the
White House. After leaving Washington, Mrs. Ford
was treated for and successfully battled alcohol
and prescription drug abuse. She was candid
about her addictions and went on to establish the
Betty Ford Center, which is recognized as the
country's premier treatment facility. Her second
book, *Betty: A Glad Awakening*, outlines her
recovery process. Today, she actively serves as
the chairperson of the board of directors of the
center.

———————— ➔ ← ————————

"My whole focus," Mrs. Ford remembered, "was pretty much learning about government and politics, because I had not been aware of how government really operated in depth to any extent. This was my husband's new career, and I thought I should find out about it. . . . I did all the things that a political wife should participate in. I went to speakers' clubs to learn how to speak—it was almost the chic thing to do. And I was—as far as the Republicans were concerned—instigating some of their activities."

❧

In the course of her vigorous efforts to get the Equal Rights Amendment ratified, Mrs. Ford was asked by Washington journalist Myra MacPherson if she pushed her point of view with her husband. "If he doesn't get it in the office in the day," she said, laughing, "he gets it in the ribs at night."

❧

Mr. Ford spent a great deal of time traveling, not just during his years as President, but throughout his marriage to Mrs. Ford. In fact, Mrs. Ford was so unaccustomed to having him around that she told *Vogue* magazine, "I wake up in the middle of the night and say to him, 'What are *you* doing here?'"

❧

"I've worked hard on my husband."

❧

"Any woman who feels confident in herself and happy in what she is doing is a liberated woman."

❧

When a bold reporter asked how often she slept with her husband, Mrs. Ford cheerfully replied, "As often as possible."

❧

Her infamous use of painkillers and alcohol to get her through the White House years increased after her husband's retirement from public office. "The truth is," she said several years later, "I was at the end of my rope."

❧

Not long into her tenure as First Lady, Mrs. Ford realized, "I'd come to recognize more clearly the power of the woman in the White House . . . a power which could be used to help."

❧

She described the First Lady's duties as "much more than a twenty-four-hour job than anyone would guess" and said of previous First Ladies, "now that I realize what they've had to put up with, I have new respect and admiration for every one of them."

❧

The Smithsonian Institution's "First Ladies" exhibit soon became the most popular of them all. When it was redesigned in the early 1990s to

stress actions rather than gowns, it drew even
more crowds. Mrs. Ford applauded the change:
"Now I will be remembered for what I did, rather
than what I wore."

Rosalynn Carter

b. 1927

First Lady
JANUARY 20, 1977–JANUARY 20, 1981

Rosalynn Eleanor Smith Carter grew up as a neighbor to the Carter family in the small town of Plains, Georgia. After her father's death, she worked with her mother as a seamstress to support the family. She married Jimmy Carter once he graduated from the U.S. Naval Academy in 1946. They traveled to different naval stations until Mr. Carter left the service to run the family peanut, fertilizer, and seed business upon his father's death. Mrs. Carter worked full time with her husband during this period.

After Mr. Carter entered politics in the 1960s, Mrs. Carter campaigned for him wholeheartedly and even traveled alone to drum up support for him during his presidential bid. As First Lady, she advised her husband in almost all matters, and she attended major briefings and cabinet meetings. She supported the performing arts but centered her efforts on programs that benefited victims of mental illness. She served as the honorary chairperson of the President's Commission on Mental Health. Rosalynn Carter currently works at the Carter Center, an organization that promotes worldwide peace and human rights, to advocate greater access to mental health care. She wrote her best-selling autobiography, *First Lady from Plains*, after retiring to her hometown.

"I was *determined* to be taken seriously."

"I don't mind being called tough. I am strong. I do have definite ideas and opinions. In the sense that 'tough' means that I can take a lot, stand up to a lot, it's a fair description."

Mrs. Carter eventually controlled the books for Carter's peanut business. "After a few years, I was explaining some things to him. I knew more about . . . the business on paper than Jimmy did. I knew which parts of the business were profitable, which were not, how much money we had, how much credit, and how much we owed on our debts. We grew together—as full partners."

～

Previous First Ladies had occasionally traveled abroad by themselves, but their missions had been primarily ceremonial. When it became clear to a reporter that the purpose of Mrs. Carter's Latin American tour was to talk about important matters of state with the leaders of other lands, he challenged her. "You have neither been elected by the American people nor confirmed by the Senate to discuss foreign policy with the heads of [other countries]. Do you consider this trip an appropriate exercise of your position?"

Her reply helped earn her the moniker "Steel Magnolia Blossom": "I am the person closest to the President of the United States," she said sharply, "and if I can explain his policies and let the people of Latin America know of his great interest and friendship, I intend to do so."

～

Even though Mr. Carter never got the opportunity to appoint a Supreme Court Justice, "it was always understood between us," Mrs. Carter said, "that a woman would be appointed if a vacancy occurred."

⸘

Mrs. Carter wrote: "I remember a friend of the Kennedys once saying that it was odd to be upstairs in the private family rooms and hear the shuffle of people's feet from the White House tours going on below. In the Governor's Mansion (in Georgia), well, there was no way for me to get out of that house except through the main halls. We lived on the second floor there, too, so it was the same situation as here. Except that here you can come and go privately.

"One time here, though, I did get caught. I wanted to press a dress—just quickly. I had on my blue bathrobe and I went down with the dress over my arm and suddenly a group of sightseers came around the corner and there I was!"

⸘

After the election results showed a clear victory for Ronald Reagan, a reporter watching the returns with the Carters commented, "Mr. President, you're a great example. You don't seem bitter at all." Mrs. Carter burst out, "I'm bitter enough for both of us."

⸘

She later remarked, "I won't say it's a relief not to be the First Lady, because I enjoyed every minute of it."

NANCY REAGAN

b. 1921

First Lady

JANUARY 20, 1981–JANUARY 20, 1989

Anne Frances "Nancy" Robbins Davis Reagan studied drama at Smith College before becoming a professional stage actress. She eventually acted in eleven films; her last was *Hellcats of the Navy*, with her husband Ronald Reagan. She met the native Californian actor when he was president of the Screen Actors

Guild. Soon after their 1952 marriage, she retired
from acting. She expressed her devotion to her
family, which would eventually include a daughter
and a son, in saying, "A woman's real happiness
and real fulfillment come from within the home
with her husband and children."

Mrs. Reagan raised national awareness of drug
and alcohol abuse while serving as First Lady during the 1980s with her "Just Say No" campaign.
She often visited the elderly, the handicapped, and
veterans while her husband was Governor of
California, and she continued to support those
groups while in the White House. Mrs. Reagan is a
breast cancer survivor. She now lives in retirement with her husband and has published an
autobiography entitled *My Turn: The Memoirs of
Nancy Reagan.*

Mrs. Reagan asserts that the ideals of love, self-
lessness, and honesty "have endured because
they are right and are no less right today than
yesterday."

On her film career: "Most of [those movies]
are best forgotten."

"I had no desire to continue as an actress once
I became a wife . . . I had seen too many mar-
riages fall apart when the wife continued her
career. I knew it wouldn't be possible for me to

have the kind of marriage I wanted—and Ronnie wanted, though he never asked me to give it up—if I continued my acting career."

❧

Her adoring gaze toward her husband unnerved even some of her friends. "Nancy, people just don't *believe* it when you look at Ronnie that way—as though you are saying, 'He's my hero.'"

"But he *is* my hero," she exclaimed.

❧

"I sometimes had the feeling that if it was raining outside, it was probably my fault. [Of course] based on the press reports I read . . . I wouldn't have liked me either."

❧

"My life began when I got married."

❧

The day after Mr. Reagan was shot in 1981, Frank Sinatra rushed to his hospital bedside. Mrs. Reagan greeted him by exclaiming, "Frank! Thank God you're here. There's finally someone I can tell my dirty stories to!"

❧

Soviet Foreign Minister Andrey Gromyko was chatting amiably with Mrs. Reagan at the White House when he suddenly turned serious. "Does your husband believe in peace or war?" he asked.

"Peace," she replied.

"You are sure?"

"Yes."

"Well," he said, "you whisper peace in his ear every night."

"I will," she promised. Then she added, "I'll also whisper it in your ear."

ॐ

"For eight years, I was sleeping with the President, and if that doesn't give you special access, I don't know what does."

ॐ

Responding to insinuations that she made her husband look like a wimp by meddling in affairs of state, she quipped, "This morning I had planned to clear up U.S.–Soviet differences on intermediate-range nuclear missiles. But I decided to clean out Ronnie's sock drawer instead."

ॐ

Rumors of her domination persisted. She tried to set the record straight by giving a speech to newspaper publishers at the end of her husband's second term. She began by joking that she had almost had to cancel. "You know how busy I am," she said. "I'm staffing the White House and over-seeing arms talks. I'm writing speeches."

Then she became serious. "Although I don't get involved in policy, it's silly to suggest that my opinion should not carry some weight with a man I've been married to for thirty-five years. I'm a woman who loves her husband and I make no apologies for looking out for his personal and political welfare. . . . I have opinions, he has opinions. We don't always agree. But neither marriage nor politics denies a spouse the right to hold an opinion and the right to expose it."

༽

Her advice to future First Ladies: "Once you're in the White House, don't think it's going to be a glamorous, fairy-tale life. It's very hard work with high highs and low lows. Since you're under a microscope, everything is magnified, so just keep your perspective and your patience."

BARBARA BUSH

b. 1925

First Lady

JANUARY 20, 1989–JANUARY 20, 1993

*B*arbara Pierce Bush, the great-great-great niece of fourteenth U.S. President Franklin Pierce, married George H. W. Bush while he was home on leave during World War II. After moving to Texas, Mrs. Bush gave birth to and raised six children while her husband made his mark in the oil industry. He later served in various political and public positions, causing the family to move twenty-nine times in forty-four years.

Mrs. Bush's straightforward, relaxed manner evoked a warm reception from the American public when she became First Lady in 1989. She calls her image that of "everybody's grandmother." Mrs. Bush attributes her popularity to three traits: "I'm fair and I like children and I adore my husband." Her love of children prompted her to crusade for the promotion of literacy as "the most important issue we have." She is honorary chair of the Barbara Bush Foundation for Family Literacy, which was launched in 1989. Proceeds from her two books, written from the point of view of her dogs, have gone to the various charities that Mrs. Bush supports. She is involved in fund-raising for the effort to cure leukemia, the disease that claimed her daughter Robin's life when the girl was four years old.

Did Mrs. Bush regret dropping out of college to get married? "No regrets," she insisted. "If I had, I could have gone back to school. I think people who tell you they have regrets are dumb."

She summed up her existence in Texas in the 1950s and 1960s as an era of "diapers, runny noses, earaches, more Little League games than you could believe possible; and those unscheduled races to the hospital emergency room; Sunday school and church; of hours of urging homework, of short chubby arms around your neck and sticky kisses."

It was also a period "of experiencing bumpy moments—not many, but a few—of feeling that I'd never, ever be able to have fun again, and coping with the feeling that George Bush, in his excitement of starting a small company and traveling around the world, was having a lot of fun."

ᎫᏢ

Mrs. Bush once admitted that she'd taken up needlepoint in the White House "just to keep from looking and feeling bored to death" while listening to a repetitious speech.

ᎫᏢ

The outspoken Mrs. Bush once famously referred to the Democratic candidate for Vice President, Geraldine Ferraro, as "a four-million-dollar . . . I can't say it, but it rhymes with rich."

ᎫᏢ

As she ascended to First Ladyhood, Barbara Bush remarked, "My mail tells me that a lot of fat, white-haired, wrinkled ladies are tickled pink."

ᎫᏢ

"I don't fool around with [George Bush's] office, and he doesn't fool around with my household."

ᎫᏢ

She told Wellesley College's graduating class of 1990: "Who knows? Somewhere out there in this audience may even be someone who will one day follow in my footsteps and preside over the White House as the President's spouse. And . . . I wish him well."

~

Unlike a great many of her predecessors, Mrs. Bush made no secret of enjoying her position as First Lady. "I love living here," she often told people. "You'd be an awfully spoiled person if you didn't love this life."

~

In the preface to her memoir, Mrs. Bush wrote, "No man, woman, or child ever had a better life." In telling her life story, she used the word "wonderful" so many times that her editor restricted her to use the word only once on each page.

~

"You really only have two choices: You can like what you do, *or* you can dislike it. I choose to like it, and what fun I've had."

HILLARY RODHAM CLINTON

b. 1947

First Lady
JANUARY 20, 1993–JANUARY 20, 2001

illary Diane Rodham Clinton excelled at Wellesley College and went on to Yale Law School, where she met her future husband, Bill Clinton. While at law school, she developed her enduring commitment to advocating the rights of children and families. She married Mr. Clinton in 1975 and they each began teaching law at the University of Arkansas in Fayetteville. Mrs. Clinton was honored as Arkansas Woman of the Year in 1983 and Young Mother of the Year in 1984 (her daughter Chelsea was born in 1980) in recognition of her professional and personal achievements and her work in the community. During her twelve years as the Governor's wife, she followed the advice that she often gave to others "to find the right balance in our lives." She worked as a full-time partner in a law firm—twice earning the *National Law Journal*'s nod as "One of the 100 Most Influential Lawyers in America"—while fulfilling social duties and continuing to fight for the rights of children and families.

Mrs. Clinton's activist lifestyle caused her to reject the traditional role of the First Lady as a silent partner. She traveled extensively, including a trip to Beijing for the United Nations Fourth World Conference on Women. Her husband assigned her to head up the national task force on health care, but the bill that resulted from her work was rejected, and from then on the First Lady, though no less politically active, refrained from any further involvement in policy. In 1996 Mrs. Clinton became the first First Lady to testify to a grand jury. She was summoned regarding the Clintons' possible connection to a financial scandal called the Whitewater Affair. She wrote the book *It Takes a Village* to explain the community's responsibility for children. While still First Lady, Mrs. Clinton established residency in Chappaqua, New York, so that she could run for New York Senator. She won the election in 2000.

The first student ever to speak at a Wellesley College commencement, she shocked the audience of parents, classmates, and faculty in 1969 by tossing aside her opening remarks and openly chiding the preceding speaker, Republican Senator Edward William Brooke III of Massachusetts. He had said that while he believed that "productive dissent" was fundamental in a thriving democracy, he rebuked "self-proclaimed radicals" who were "merely exploiting issues for the sake of some ulterior purpose, and their "primitive breast-beating" made them responsible for the outbreak of student protests throughout the country.

Mrs. Rodham, then twenty-one and president of the student government, was then introduced by Wellesley's president, Ruth Adams.

I am very glad that Miss Adams made it clear that what I am speaking for today is all of us—the four hundred of us—and I find myself in a familiar position, that of reacting, something that our generation has been doing for quite a while now. We're not in the positions yet of leadership and power, but we do have that indispensable task of criticizing and constructive protest, and I find myself reacting just briefly to some of the things that Senator Brooke said. This has to be brief because I do have a little speech to give.

Part of the problem with empathy with professed goals is that empathy doesn't do us anything. We've had lots of empathy, we've had lots of sympathy, but we feel that for too long our leaders have used politics as the art of the possible. And the challenge now is to practice politics as the art of making what appears to be impossible, possible.

The question about possible and impossible was one that we brought with us to Wellesley four years ago. We arrived not yet knowing what was not possible. Consequently, we expected a lot. Our attitudes are easily understood, having grown up, having come to consciousness in the first five years of this decade—years dominated by men with dreams, men in the civil rights movement, the Peace Corps, the space program—so we arrived at Wellesley and we found, as all of us have found, that there was a gap between expectation and realities. But it wasn't a discouraging gap, and it didn't turn us into cynical, bitter old women at the age of eighteen. It just inspired us to do something about that gap. What we did is often difficult for some people to understand. They ask us quite often, "Why, if you're dissatisfied, do you stay in a place?" Well, if you didn't care a lot about it you wouldn't stay. It's almost as though my mother used to say, "I'll always love you, but there are times when I certainly won't like you." Our love for this place, this particular place, Wellesley College, coupled with our freedom from the burden of an inauthentic reality, allowed us to question basic assumptions underlying our education.

Before the days of media-orchestrated demonstrations, we had our own gathering in Founder's parking lot. We protested against the rigid academic distribution requirement. We worked for a pass-fail system. We worked for a say in some of the process of academic decision-making. And luckily we were in a place where, when we questioned the meaning of a liberal arts education, there were people with enough imagination to respond to that questioning. So we have made progress. We have achieved some of the things that we initially saw as lacking in that gap between expectation and reality. Our concerns were not, of course, solely academic as all of us know. We worried about— inside Wellesley—questions of admissions, the kind of people that were coming to Wellesley, the process for getting them here. We questioned about what responsibility we should have both for our lives as individuals and for our lives as members of a collective group.

Many of the issues that I've mentioned—those of sharing power and responsibility, those of assuming power and responsibility—have been general concerns on campuses throughout the world. But underlying those concerns there is a theme, a theme which is so trite and so old because the words are so familiar. It talks about integrity and trust and respect. Words have a funny way of trapping our minds on the way to our tongues, but there are necessary means even in this multimedia age for attempting to come to grasps with some of the inarticulate—maybe inarticulable—things that we're feeling. We are, all of us, exploring a world that none of us understands and attempting to create within that uncertainty. But there are some things we feel, feelings that our prevailing, acquisitive, and competitive corporate life, including, tragically, the universities, is not the way of life for us. We're searching for more immediate, ecstatic, and penetrating modes of living. And so our questions, our questions about our institutions, about our colleges, about our churches, about our government, continue. The questions about those institutions are familiar to all of us. We have seen them heralded across the newspapers. Senator Brooke has suggested some of them this

morning. But along with using these words—
integrity, trust, and respect—in regard to
institutions and leaders, we're perhaps harsh-
est with them in regard to ourselves.

Every protest, every dissent, whether it's
an individual academic paper, or a Founder's
parking lot demonstration, is unabashedly an
attempt to forge an identity in this particular
age. That attempt at forging for many of us
over the past four years has meant coming to
terms with our humanness. Within the context of a society that we perceive—now, we
can talk about reality, and I would like to talk
about reality sometime, authentic reality,
inauthentic reality, and what we have to
accept of what we see—but our perception of
it is that it hovers often between the possibility of disaster and the potentiality for imagi-
natively responding to men's needs. There's a
very strange conservative strain that goes
through a lot of the New Left, collegiate
protests that I find very intriguing because it
hearkens back to a lot of the old virtues, to
the fulfillment of original ideas. And it's also
a very unique American experience. It's such
a great adventure. If the experiment in
human living doesn't work in this country, in
this age, it's not going to work anywhere.

But we also know that to be educated,
the goal of it must be human liberation, a liberation enabling each of us to fulfill our

capacity so as to be free to create within and around ourselves. To be educated to freedom must be evidenced in action, and here again is where we ask ourselves, as we have asked our parents and our teachers, questions about integrity, trust, and respect. Those three words mean different things to all of us. Some of the things they can mean, for instance: integrity—the courage to be whole, to try to mold an entire person in this particular context, living in relation to one another in the full poetry of existence. If the only tool we have, ultimately, to use is our lives, so we use it in the way we can by choosing a way to live that will demonstrate the way we feel and the way we know.

Trust. This is one word that when I asked the class at our rehearsal what it was they wanted me to say for them, everyone came up to me and said, "Talk about trust, talk about the lack of trust both for us and the way we feel about others. Talk about the trust bust." What can you say about it? What can you say about a feeling that permeates a generation and that perhaps is not even understood by those who are distrusted? All they can do is keep trying again and again and again. There's that wonderful line in "East Coker" by Eliot about there's only the trying, again and again and again, to win again what we've lost before.

And then respect. There's that mutuality of respect between people where you don't see people as percentage points, where you don't manipulate people, where you're not interested in social engineering for people. The struggle for an integrated life existing in an atmosphere of communal trust and respect is one with desperately important political and social consequences. And the word *consequences* of course catapults us into the future. One of the most tragic things that happened yesterday, a beautiful day, was that I was talking to a woman who said that she wouldn't want to be me for anything in the world. She wouldn't want to live today and look ahead to what it is she sees because she's afraid. Fear is always with us, but we just don't have time for it—not now.

On what attracted her to Mr. Clinton, whom she met while at Yale Law School: "He wasn't afraid of me."

"I have always tried to listen to that voice deep inside of [me]—the voice that tells you right from wrong. It's so easy to find yourself editing feelings and beliefs based on what people may think. You only have one life to live. I knew my relationship to Bill was very important to me."

"One of the reasons I came home so much [during the 1992 campaign] was not only to see how [daughter Chelsea] was, but to recharge my batteries, which she was a big part of doing. We just spent a lot of time together, and really it was important for me. I took her to school, I took her shopping, we watched videos, we both just kind of refueled our own energy level so that we could both keep going in it."

৶৴

On her husband's decision to run for President in 1992: "[Bill and I] believe passionately in this country and we cannot stand by for one more year and watch what is happening to it."

৶৴

On campaigning: "There's not much inherent attractiveness in turning your life over to this process."

৶৴

"If you vote for my husband, you get me; it's a two-for-one, blue-plate special."

৶৴

"I have never thought that it was going to be an easy campaign, or that the kinds of issues and changes that Bill Clinton was advocating would be easily understood or accepted by everybody. . . . Remember, Abraham Lincoln was the first person who said you can't please all of the people all of the time. But what we're interested in is trying to convince a majority of Americans to understand what's at stake in this election. And I feel such a personal obligation to help my husband on this and to try to stand up and say what we think is going on in the country, and then to try to bring about changes that will help people. So I'm sure there are people who are not going to approve or understand, and I just hope that most people will listen and think, 'Why are these two doing this,' you know? 'Why is Bill Clinton putting himself on the line like this?' And it's because he's really committed to making the changes this country needs."

❧

During the 1992 campaign, Mrs. Clinton predicted: "We'll have a woman President by 2010."

She was immediately asked whether she'd consider running. "We'll talk later," she replied.

❧

Two days before her husband's inauguration, NBC anchor Tom Brokaw asked Mrs. Clinton, "What do you think you'll do the first morning you awaken in the White House and look at each other?"

"Pull the covers over our heads," Hillary replied.

❧

"There isn't really any way to prepare for it . . . when you walk in that door at the White House the day that your husband is inaugurated, you really do not know what you are walking into. You can read history, you can know that there are all kinds of experiences that people have had to go through, but until you actually are there, day in and day out, neither the wonder and the thrill and the excitement nor the challenges of it seem quite real. And it's a constant adjustment. And I think it's been an extraordinary and for me it's been a positive and wonderful experience, but I could never have predicted how I would have reacted to what would have happened to me."

༄

Shortly after taking up residence in the White House, Mrs. Clinton famously said, "I suppose I could have stayed home and baked cookies and had teas, but what I decided to do is fulfill my profession. The work that I have done as a professional, a public advocate, has been aimed . . . to assure that women can make the choices . . . whether it's a full-time career, full-time motherhood, or some combination."

༄

There was hell to pay: "Now, the fact is, I've made my share of cookies and served hundreds of cups of tea. But I never thought that made me a good, bad, or indifferent mother, or a good or bad person. So it never occurred to me that my comment would be taken as insulting mothers (I guess including my own!) who choose to stay home with their children full-time. Nor did it occur to me that the next day's headlines would reduce me to an anti-family 'career woman.'"

~

"I have yet to meet a woman who doesn't have some ambivalence. Introduce me to her, if you will, because I think most women, as they go through their lives, face a lot of tough choices," Mrs. Clinton remarked, adding "anyone who knows me, and knows the kind of work I've done now for many years, knows that part of what I'm trying to accomplish is to provide more opportunities for more women to choose that full-time homemaking and mothering role, if that's what the choice is. I think it's important for women to respect each other's choices. There are enough stresses in today's life without setting up camps against one another and pointing fingers at each other."

~

It seemed Mrs. Clinton could do no right: "You know, I'm not sitting here like some little woman standing by her man like Tammy Wynette. I'm sitting here because I love him and I respect him and I honor what he's been through and what we've been through together. And, you know, if that's not enough for people, then, heck, don't vote for him."

❧

Then: "I didn't mean to hurt Tammy Wynette as a person. I happen to be a country-western fan. If she feels like I've hurt her feelings, I'm sorry about that."

❧

Charged by her husband with supervising health care reform, she remarked along the way: "Every President who has touched [health care reform] has got burned in one way or the other because the interests involved are so powerful."

❧

"I'm not an expert on health care. I'm not somebody who has studied it or ever, you know, done any of the things that you do when you're in the system. But what I really want to do is be somebody who helps make sure that what we come up with sounds real and will work. I mean, I want it to be understandable and workable for real Americans. . . . I know how I feel about my doctors. I want to make sure that I'll always be able to have the doctors that I feel most comfortable with."

❧

"Although we are the richest country in the world and we have the best of medical care available in the world, we spend more money on health care and take care of fewer people than our competitors, who provide health care to all of

the people and have better outcomes for the
money that they spend on it. What we have
instead is a patchwork nonsystem."

کئ

"Until we have everybody in the system, we
will not be able to control health care costs."

کئ

"I really love [the White House], and I love the
idea that not only the Presidents and their families
but literally millions and millions of Americans
have walked these halls and come to receptions
and taken a tour. You know, it's the only house of
a head of state anywhere in the world that's open
to the public. You can't go to any other country
and have the accessibility to this kind of a place
except here in America."

کئ

From a speech given at George Washington
University in 1994: "I frankly have gotten a little
frustrated and itchy being in the White House
because I feel cut off from people, and I feel that
I'm not really out there doing what I care about
and making a contribution. I've always been very
involved in any community I've ever lived in. I've
actually been trying to think about how I could be
better integrated into my community, which is
Washington now."

کئ

"I don't think there's anything that has happened to me that is, frankly, very new."

❧

"I don't even read what people mostly say about me."

❧

"I apparently remind people of their mother-in-law or their boss, or something."

❧

"I have read enough history to know that no matter what I do, I will be fair game."

❧

"I'm not a behind-the-scenes kind of person. I'm very overt."

❧

"You can be very involved and on the front lines like Mrs. Roosevelt and be criticized. Or you can be totally concerned with your family and not venture forth and be criticized. It is a no-win situation."

❧

"If we ever want to get [the war in] Bosnia off the front page, all I have to do is . . . change my hair and we'll all be occupied with something else."

❧

During her keynote address at Scripps College in April 1994, Mrs. Clinton reflected, "I'm often asked if what I am doing in Washington creates a new role model for First Ladies. And I always say I don't want to create any new stereotype. I want to free women to live according to their own needs and desires. I do not want to create a new category that anyone after me must somehow fit into. I want all women to be given the respect they deserve to have for the choices they may make."

❧

By 1995, she and her family had become a good deal more acclimated to life in Washington in general, and in the White House in particular. Mrs. Clinton noted, "we have had some funny experiences in the past three years or so, where, you know, my husband will say, 'Gee, I want a banana,' and next thing you know there are bananas everywhere. So . . . we have learned to be . . . maybe a little bit more careful about that."

❧

When asked to name her most rewarding moments after more than three years as First Lady, Mrs. Clinton immediately said, "The passage of the Brady Bill. And the ban on assault weapons."

❧

She told the Greater Detroit Chamber of Commerce in 1995: "The best social program is a job. The best social policy is a robust economy.

But one does not live by jobs and the economy alone. There is also a spiritual dimension to life. There is a sense of connection to life."

⌇

Mrs. Clinton is a great admirer of Eleanor Roosevelt. "She was often attacked and criticized, but there was never any confusion in her own mind about what constituted a meaningful life. She refused to be categorized or stereotyped, which, of course, greatly frustrated her critics. She was one of those rare people who strike that elusive balance between 'me' and 'we.' Between our rights and expectations as individuals and our obligations to the larger community. She considered herself as a citizen. Someone who was there trying to make sure that democracy worked well. Someone who wanted to help educate other citizens about what they could do."

⌇

Bob Woodward posited in his book *The Choice* that Mrs. Clinton held imaginary conversations with Eleanor Roosevelt. "I try to figure out what she would do in my shoes. She usually responds by telling me to buck up or at least to grow skin as thick as a rhinoceros."

At a Nashville conference on families, Mrs. Clinton laughingly mocked the very notion of these imaginary conversations. "Shortly before I arrived, I had one of my conversations with Mrs. Roosevelt and she thinks this is a terrific idea as well."

⤳

On Chelsea's life in the White House: "She's
a happy teenager, I think. She comes and goes
pretty much as she pleases; she has wonderful
friends. We've kept the press out of her life. That
may be our only achievement so far!"

⤳

During the 1996 campaign: "I think that unfortunately a lot of our campaigns have gotten nasty
and mean-spirited in the past years. Well, I think
it's because when people do not have their own
vision for what this country should do, don't have
a positive program to help people get and keep
jobs or provide health care, or better education, or
keep the environment clean, then you're more
likely to see a campaign based on personality. And
I don't think that that's good news, but I hope that
the American people will see it for what it is. And
I have a lot of confidence in the American public
and expect that will be what they'll do."

⤳

"I never believe in polls—good, bad, indifferent."

⤳

"I sometimes don't know what I've been accused of from day to day."

⤳

"If people disagree with one another, let's do it

in a civil, polite way. Let's not call each other names. Let's try to agree that our most important effort should be coming together to help each other. And so then I think the criticism, whether it's directed at me or anybody else, it's not going to count for very much."

⳾

"I love watching the Republicans squirm when the tables are turned. They are great at dishing it out, but they really can't take it when the truth is pointed out about them."

⳾

"We have such a schizophrenic view toward politics—people claim they want somebody to tell them the truth, to be tough, make hard decisions. But they don't want it to be painful. Reagan had such a hold on the popular imagination, he could have asked something from people, but he squandered an extraordinary political opportunity.

"At least he had some core beliefs. They defied logic, but at least he had them. He was followed by someone who didn't."

⳾

"It is such hypocrisy for some people in this town [Washington, D.C.] to yell about our movies when we use sex to sell everything in America."

⳾

On her book *It Takes a Village:* "[I hope it] will remind us that for America to be a strong, confident country, we have to start caring for our children as if we were a village in the very best sense of the word."

⨾

"I don't use [the term First Lady] much personally, but I don't object to people using it because it is a tradition that we think started with Martha Washington. So, it's not the term so much, it's the expectations that surround the role that I find fascinating. I have spent a lot of time in the last several years reading about my predecessors and have discovered that nearly every one of them had a kind of bumpy time here because there's really no way to satisfy the extraordinary expectations that are put upon the person who is married to the President. And it has been both somewhat sustained, if you will, as well as a cautionary tale to realize that the women who have been here before have encountered many different kinds of challenges. And at the end of the day, you have to be yourself, you have to say and stand up for what you believe in, you have to be willing to get up and go ahead and take the slings and arrows and just try to persist through them, because it's apparently an inevitable part of our American democracy."

⨾

"I believe with all my heart that women are the world's greatest untapped resource, and that that resource is too often being wasted today, but that each of us in our own lives and in the lives of those we can touch can begin to unleash the full power and glory of that resource."

↝

"On the eve of this new century and millennium, our task as Americans is to work together to perfect our union, just as those before us have done. Our task is to respect our political process and our democratic institutions and respect each other when we feel strongly opposed to points of view, nevertheless to treat each other with civility. Because we know we are granted privileges and rights here in this country that others have died for and continue to die for."

↝

"Our lives are a mixture of different roles," Mrs. Clinton once said. "Most of us are doing the best we can to find whatever the right balance is for our lives. For me the elements of that balance are family, work, and service."

↝

"I have a burning desire to do what I can, a desire to make the world around me—kind of going out in concentric circles—better for everybody."

LAURA BUSH

b. 1946

First Lady
JANUARY 20, 2001–

*L*aura *Welch* *Bush*'s life has been dedicated to the cause of education. The native Texan obtained her bachelor's degree in education and her master's degree in library science. She taught in public schools for nine years before marrying George W. Bush in her hometown of Midland, Texas, in 1977. In 1998, she

launched a program to help young children prepare for school. She organized the first annual
Texas Book Festival to raise funds for Texas public
libraries. Mrs. Bush also is active in women's
health issues, especially breast cancer awareness.
She serves on several committees, including the
national Reading Is Fundamental Advisory
Council and the Information Science Foundation
Advisory Council.

"Most people don't know anything about me, but
based on the things that have been published,
people probably think I'm a shy librarian. Lonely,
an only child. Well," she laughs, "very few librari-
ans fit the stereotype: They're people who like
knowledge and are interested in a *lot* of different
things."

"When your husband is running for President,
it's a really good thing if you're not that anxious."

"My husband told me I'd never have to make a
political speech," she told an audience for one of
her early political addresses. "So much for political promises."

Still, "The political races were the times
[George and I] grew closest to each other."

She laughingly told sorority sisters at Southern Methodist University, "I have to practice my Miss America wave. . . . You just never know when it will come in handy." She raised her hand, middle fingers together, and moved it in a mechanical gesture. One of those friends now says, "When we see her on television before she gets into a car or as she walks to the stage, we'll scream, 'Look! She's doing her Miss America wave!'"

≫

"I'm not a worrier. I think it's just a temperament. People are born with their temperament, and I have that."

≫

"We have a life, friends and family outside politics. We'll stay the same people, no matter what happens," Mrs. Bush asserted during her husband's bid for the White House. "But this is going to be a great adventure, win or lose."

≫

On her husband's famous drinking problem: "I think he was drinking too much," she admits. "It was not affecting our lives—he never drank during the day, just at night. But I think he realized it was counterproductive. George loves to give me credit for helping him to quit, but the fact is, he has a lot of discipline."

≫

"[George] adds a lot of excitement to my life. I think that's one of the reasons I was attracted to

him. He was high-energy and fun and had a great
sense of humor. He still makes me laugh a lot.
That's very relaxing, I have to say. It's such a great
personality trait; it sort of defuses tension. And
with the kids, when they were upset or worried or
groping, a daddy who could be funny and make
faces and have costumes, I think it's a wonderful
gift. His dad was the same way."

⤳

On problem-solving with her husband: "We
talk things out, but neither one of us really ago-
nizes over decisions. For instance, things about
the new house we're building—we don't agonize
over it. Which I like. I mean, I like the way
George is decisive. Because I'm like that too. I
don't want to spend a lot of time worrying about
some decision, or second-guessing."

⤳

"We made a real effort for our children to
have a normal life. We were living in Dallas when
George's dad was President, and they went to a
public school until the sixth grade. We moved to
Austin when George was elected [Governor], and
they went to a private school—a great Episcopal
school. Then they chose to go to public school,
the big downtown-Austin high school. We have
not ever used them in any of our political ads.
They've never had to go to any political events.
We felt like if we protected them from that, it was
more likely they would have a normal life. In

Texas we specifically asked the media to give our children every courtesy and privacy, and they have—in general."

༖

"I hope [our daughters] will be happy and have loving relationships. There are different types of relationships: with friends, with spouses, and with your children. I want them to have all of those. And I hope they find some sort of job or profession or service they like. I had jobs that were traditionally 'women's jobs'—librarian, teacher—but that's really what I had wanted to do. I hope they have the opportunity to have whatever job they want."

༖

"If [parents] just would try [reading to their children] once, they'd find it not only relaxes their child, it relaxes them. I know how busy families are, and how many demands are on mothers, but there are also so few years between when a child is born and when he starts school that I hope parents will just take those few minutes as often as they can.

"Not only is it great for brain development and gives a child a big advantage when he starts school because of a larger vocabulary, it's also great for making loving memories. I have this big Texas book festival in Austin that's a fundraiser for public libraries, and almost to a person, every professional writer (who attends) had a mother or dad who loved to read to them. That shows just how important reading is at home."

࿎

Recalling her father-in-law's presidential campaign in 1992, Laura Bush said, "I realized there was an image out there that was *not* him. That worried me, and it was one reason I think I was reluctant when people started talking about George running for President. We talked about that. Because you don't like to see someone characterized in a way that you know they're not. Of course, in a very partisan political race, your opponents will try to paint a picture of you that's not true. There is labeling and stereotyping. And the way the press reports things, people look one-dimensional, and everyone is really much more complicated than that."

࿎

"Barbara Bush—there's a perception of her as grandmotherly, sweet, the baking-cookies type. Which of course she is, but she's *fun.* She's entertaining, a great storyteller. She's the one you want to sit by at the dinner party."

࿎

"I have learned so much from watching [Barbara Bush]. About what it is like to live in a public house like this one. Things that have to do with how you raise your children. And she does give me advice. When there were the debates in

New Hampshire last year, she said, 'Now you know all the candidates' wives will be there, and it's best if you are the first one to speak.' I mean, it wouldn't have occurred to me. It shows what an advantage I have to have her as my mother-in-law."

⌇

"I have a lifelong passion for introducing children to the magic of words. I was a public school teacher and I know what a difficult and rewarding job teaching is. I am proud of my efforts on behalf of the children of Texas and I look forward to building those efforts on behalf of all American schoolchildren."

⌇

"I think a great teacher is priceless. I think teachers have a more profound impact on our society and culture than any other profession. Do [teachers] make enough money? No, of course not. Bond elections come before school districts and a lot of times they're defeated. We need to make sure everybody realizes how important it is to recruit and keep really great teachers in our schools."

⌇

"We certainly need to recruit new teachers. Teachers should be paid more. We need to look at school buildings and make sure they're safe, that they are an environment that we would want our children to spend their time in. . . . Parents can help landscape schools and make sure they look really good for children."

❧

Pondering the Littleton, Colorado, school disaster and other tragic instances in which students opened fire on classmates, Mrs. Bush concluded firmly, "Schools could be smaller. When they were small enough that nearly every teacher at least recognized nearly every student, that helped."

❧

"I had the luxury of staying home with my children. I know that I was lucky to be able to do that. But I also think that if we got to a point where our government paid for things (like paid parenting leave), we'd end up losing certain freedoms. There'd be all sorts of regulations about what you could do while you stayed home with your child. And I really don't think Americans want that."

❧

On her impending ascent onto the national stage, she said, in January 1999, "I'm reluctant. Absolutely. It's a major life change. I'm not particularly worried about safety. Privacy. I'm very worried about privacy."

❧

The self-described "introvert" says simply that she is "interested in politics because my husband is involved in politics."

۞

"I've never really been that interested in clothes," she told *People* magazine in November 1999. "Before I had the job as the First Lady of Texas, I wore jeans, pants, and T-shirts. So I got a new wardrobe—suits, jackets, skirts, and pant sets."

۞

On the presidential campaign trail, Mrs. Bush was overheard telling her husband, "Rein it in, Bubba," when he began pontificating.

۞

Mrs. Bush told an audience at an event celebrating the writers and teachers of America on January 19, 2001, "Though I haven't planned a lesson plan in a long time, I will always have tremendous respect for the teachers all across America." She quipped that the day's event was "a librarian's dream," because "not only do we get to hear from five respected American authors but also, if anybody in the audience starts to get rowdy, I get to tell them to hush up."

۞

Not adhering to his father's pronounced aversion, George W. will eat broccoli, Mrs. Bush explained, "as long as you only give him the tops and not the stalks and especially if it has a great cheese sauce." Another gustatory change in the White House after Clinton: the kitchen closes at dinner time, not at midnight. (Clinton is a well-known snacker.) Mrs. Bush explained that the new closing time is "just to protect ourselves and our weight." Meanwhile, she has been forced, for obvious reasons, to abandon her favorite form of exercise: walking. She said she keeps intending to use the White House exercise room, but "so far I haven't quite made it there. I need to get on the treadmill. I better get on the treadmill."

꩜

The nation was fairly startled to learn after the inauguration that Laura Bush is pro-choice. "No, I don't think [Roe v. Wade] should be overturned," she said during an interview on the *Today* show. "We should do what we can to limit the number of abortions," she continued, by "talking about responsibility with boys and girls, by teaching abstinence, having abstinence classes every-where, in schools and in churches and in Sunday schools."

꩜

"The role of the First Lady is whatever the First Lady wants it to be."

BIBLIOGRAPHY

PRIMARY SOURCES

Adler, Bill, editor. *The Common Sense of Three First Ladies*. New York: The Citadel Press, 1966.

——. *The Uncommon Wisdom of Jacqueline Kennedy: A Portrait in Her Own Words*. New York: The Citadel Press, 1994.

Anthony, Carl Sferrazza. *First Ladies: The Saga of the Presidents' Wives and Their Power, 1789–1961*. New York: Quill/Morrow, 1993.

Caroli, Betty Boyd. *America's First Ladies*. New York: The Reader's Digest Association, 1996.

Carroll, Andrew, editor. *Letters of a Nation*. New York: Broadway Books, 1999.

Hay, Peter. *All the Presidents' Ladies: Anecdotes of the Women behind the Men in the White House*. New York: Viking, 1988.

Klapthor, Margaret Brown. *The First Ladies Cook Book*. New York: Parents Magazine Press, 1964.

Mayo, Edith P., general editor. *The Smithsonian Book of the First Ladies: Their Lives, Times, and Issues*. New York: Henry Holt and Co., 1996.

Torricelli, Robert, editor. *In Our Own Words: Extraordinary Speeches of the American Century*. New York: Kodansha International, 1999.

INDEX

INDEX